THE MESSIANIC GENEALOGY OF JESUS CHRIST

The Called and Predestined Progenitors Constituting the Davidic
Divine Genealogy of the Son Of Man: The Mashiach

Ayuba Mshelia

authorHOUSE®

AuthorHouse™
1663 Liberty Drive
Bloomington, IN 47403
www.authorhouse.com
Phone: 833-262-8899

Published by AuthorHouse 12/22/2020

ISBN: 978-1-6655-0976-3 (sc)
ISBN: 978-1-6655-1121-6 (e)

KJV - King James Version
Scripture taken from the King James Version of the Bible.

NASB
Scripture quotations marked NASB are taken from the New American Standard Bible®, Copyright © 1960, 1962, 1963, 1968, 1971, 1972, 1973, 1975, 1977, 1995 by The Lockman Foundation. Used by permission.

CONTENTS

PREFACE

I must acknowledge the anxiety and the exegetical Scriptural fear that overwhelmed me when the idea came to me overnight to write a booklet about the genealogy of the **Son of Man**, Jesus Christ. I was disabled by the feeling of insufficiency when the thought occurred to me—until I read 1 Cor. 8:2, which states, "If any man think that he knoweth anything, he knoweth nothing yet as he ought to know" (KJV), and 2Cor.3:5 which almost verbally states "Not that we are sufficient of ourselves to think anything as of ourselves, but our sufficiency is of God"

This apt statement from St. Paul, an Apostle of Christ, gave me the confidence I needed. I convinced myself that if I am worthy of his grace to write about the genealogy of his son, Jesus Christ, then my sufficiency must have been sufficient for him, who above all is the source and embodiment of all knowledge.

With the impetus of his divine grace and guide—and with a statement from Phil. 3:16, which reminds us to "keep living by that same standard to which we have attained" (NASB)—I was emboldened to sit down and embark on the project of writing about the genealogy of the son of God, Jesus Christ, the Messiah/Mashiach.

To me, it is a true adventure into the unknown. I'm a Christian, and always have been, but never thought I would one day have the knowledge or expertise and audacity to write a scriptural paper, let alone one about the divine Messianic line of the son of God, whom I worship and adore as a personal savior and redeemer. My exposure to the Bible and religious studies, other than as a regular Christian and Bible reader, was a brief frolic reading for the GCE Advance-level exam paper (I never sat for the exam itself as my priorities changed).

My prime objective is to harmonize the genealogy story presented by the two preeminent Evangelists, Matthew (1:1-16) and Luke (3:23-37). The two presentations use different formats and begin recording with different origins. The evangelist Luke begins with Jesus Christ himself and ascends to Adam. Matthew starts from Abraham and descends to Jesus Christ.

In the coming presentation, both directions and starting points are harmonized. Both genealogies start from Adam and descend to Jesus Christ after collapsing for many generations. The differences in their presumed audiences, however, is left unchanged. Matthew seemed to write to a Jewish audience, thereby emphasizing Christ's royal lineage through Joseph. Luke, on the other hand, wrote to a gentile audience, seemingly emphasizing Christ's legal lineage through levirate marriages through the maternal lineage of Mary, the physical daughter of Joachim, and the daughter of Heli/Eli through Panther Heli's uncle and Joachim's father.

Park (2014) states that, "The genealogy is a list of names that encapsulates and summarizes the promises of the eternal covenant and their fulfillments in light of the history of redemption" (Park, 2014; The Promise of the Eternal Covenant, pg. 10). This is important because of God's foundational planned history of redemption to send his son as a "woman's seed" (Gen. 3:15). The genealogies in both the Old and New Testament are recorded as watershed moments in God's planned redemptive history for mankind. Thus, "An era in redemptive history concludes with a genealogy; a new begins with another" (Park, ibid, pg. 10). For instance, Park (2014) observes that the genealogy in Matthew 1 is an encapsulation of God's entire history of redemption; which "proclaims that Jesus Christ is the fulfillment of every promise of the eternal covenant" (ibid); in fulfillment of Galatians 4 which states; "But when the fulness of time was come, God sent forth his Son, made of a woman, made under the law, to redeem them that were under the law, that we might receive the adoption of sons" (Gal4:4-5, KJV). The birth of Jesus Christ, the Messiah (Mashiach)—in about 4/5 BC—is the complete divine fulfillment of God's eternal covenant with man.

Even with all its inadequacies, I hope that this work will be beneficial to those who would come across it and dare open the pages to peruse its contents. I hope the harmonization of the genealogy stories of the *Son Of*

Man, true God and true Man, as presented in the Gospels of Matthew and Luke, are made succinct enough to read without trepidation.

Last but not least, I express my heartfelt gratitude to S. A. Michel, who edited the whole manuscript and gave it a beautiful, professional touch of succinctness and overall smooth, easy flow. I also must express my gratitude to Mr. Fabian McKinney of ***Olive Web Studio*** of Brooklyn, New York, and his staff of designers for reproducing an excellent adopted and greatly modified Lukan version of Levirate family tree. Last but not least my gratitude goes to Ms. Antoinette Jackson for formatting and setting everything in its rightful place.

AYM, Ph.D.
December 2020
New York

CHAPTER I

THE MESSIANIC LINE

Introduction

The Called and Predestined Progenitors Constituting the Davidic Divine Genealogy of the Son Of Man: The Mashiach

According to the Gospel of Matthew (1:1-16) and Luke (3:23-38).

The purpose of this document is twofold. Its purview is God's promise to Abraham regarding his seeds and to David regarding his Davidic Messianic patrilineal (that is, male-only) divine line, which was eventually fulfilled through the birth of the Son of God, the MESSIAH, Jesus. Secondly, it attempts to answer the question that results from the differences between the two genealogies in the Gospels of Matthew 1:1-16 and Luke 3:23-38.

The question of the qualities and characters of the individuals God chose to constitute the lineage of the **WORD** that became flesh—the Messiah, Jesus of Nazareth, the CHRIST—was one motivation that inspired my interest in the fulfillment of these divine promises.

To achieve this mundane but profound objective, we must start with the story of the first couple, Adam and Eve, who lived in the Garden of Eden. Then we proceed to God's call for Abraham, instructing him to move from Haran to Canaan, "unto a land that I will shew thee," with a promise to give him a great name, to make him a blessing, to bless those who bless him, and curse those who cursed him and finally to give him the Promised Land and through his descendants to bless all the families of the earth with a Redeemer. (Genesis 15:1-18; Genesis 12:1-9). The year God gave Abraham the promise of salvation through Jesus Christ as part of the covenant of torch in Genesis 15 can be extrapolated based on his birthdate and how old he was at the time as given in Hindson's (2013), King James Volume (KJV). *Study Bible*, to be in c. 2090 B.C. (Given that he was born in 2165 B.C. {according to Hindson, 2013, 11:26-32, pg.28} and the covenant was given when he was 75)[1]. Using a different birthdate (probably 2157 B.C.) Park gave a date of 2082 B.C. (Park, 2014, pg. 51).

We will subsequently take a cursory look at Abraham and his descendants/lineage with a return to Adam and Eve. We will trace the lineage of their son Seth directly to Abraham.

Given the number of persons involved from Adam to the fulfillment of the two promises, I can only make short and brief references to the quality of the character, shortcomings, and obedience to divine commandments (in the sight of God) of the people considered significant and God's choices for the lineage of his son, Jesus Christ.

In pursuit of uniformity and ease of reading, I've adopted Matthew's descending-order format to present the lineage in both Gospels. In 0fairness to Luke—who presents it in ascending order—I also adopted his genealogy format from Adam (the first earthly man; Genesis1:26) to Jesus (the heavenly/Spiritual man; Luke 1:26-38; Crane, 1926; Luke 1:18, 20, 23). Also, I accept Luke's coverage of the complete history of God's redemption, beginning with Adam and Eve, not Abraham, for the following reasons:

> *God first showed the path to salvation for fallen mankind through the promise of the "seed" of the woman: "I will put enmity between thee and the woman, and between thy seed*

---

[1] Born in about 2165 B.C. {Hindson, 2013, *Study Bible*, Second Edition. Nashville, TN: Thomas Nelson Publishers, 11:26-32}, promise given when 75, hence promise around 2165-75=2090 B.C.; Park A. used 2157 B.C. as the birthday, then he would arrive at 2157-75=2082 B.C. as he did {Park, 2014, *The Promise of the Eternal Covenant: God's Profound Providence as revealed in the Genealogy of Jesus Christ (The Post-Exilic Period)* North Clarendon, Vermont: Periplus Editions Publishers

and her seed; it shall bruise thy head, and thou shalt bruise his heel" (Genesis 3:15).[2]

The words "her seed" refer to Jesus Christ, who would be conceived through Mary by the Holy Spirit's power (Matthew 1:18). Christ came through Virgin Mary as a seed of the woman and not of man; "Therefore the Lord himself shall give you a sign; Behold a Virgin shall conceive, and bear a son, and shall call his name Immanuel" (Isaiah 7:14; Crane, 1926. Luke 1:30-35). The woman's seed's promise was expanded to the covenant with Noah (Genesis 6:18; 9:8-17) and with Abraham (Genesis 12:1-3; 22:15-18). It then developed into the Sinaitic covenant— a conditional covenant of works, written on a stone given to Moses on Mount Sinai and ratified there circa in either 1660 B.C. or 1652 B. C.[3] (Ex. 24:1-8; Deut. 29:1)—and, finally, to the Davidic covenant, unconditional covenant of grace based on the atoning works of Jesus Christ (Jeremiah 31:31-34; 2 Samuel 7:11-16; 1 Chronicles 17:10-14; Heb.10:16-17). Without any explanation or evidence, Park (2014) gave the Sinaitic covenant ratification date as circa 1446 B.C. (Park, pg. 51). Using this figure, he arrived at 1876 B.C. as the year the covenant was given to Abraham in Genesis 15, instead of 2090 B.C. (see footnote [1 and 2]).

All of the above covenants are eternal. They became "promises." God promised a "seed." This promise was fulfilled in Jesus Christ, and it was contained in the covenant ratified by God (Galatians 3:16-17). From the foundation of the world, God had a plan for man's redemption through his only begotten son, Jesus Christ. He manifested it in human genealogy by calling Abram to move to a new foreign land where God would make Abram's seed a chosen people out of whom God's son would become incarnate to save mankind. God could have chosen a people already

---

[2] Hindson, 2013, K.J.V., *Study Bible*, Section Edition.

[3] Park, 2014, pg. 51; According to Galatians 3:17, "and this I say, that the covenant, that was confirmed before of God in Christ, the law, which was four hundred and thirty years after, cannot disannul, that it should make the promise of none effect". Hence, if the promise was made between 2090-2082 B.C. – earlier explanation – law given 430 years later, this means it was given in either 2090-430=1660 B.C. or 2082-430=1652 B.C.

existing in Canaan, but he didn't find any worthy—hence the creation of a new people through the seed of Abraham.

This means that from Adam to Terah—father of Abram/Abraham—the human genealogy of Christ was hidden from mankind, and it was made manifest only through the call of Abraham. This implies that the sanctified[4] characters in both genealogies of Matthew and Luke's Gospels are identical from Adam to Terah and Abraham and from Abraham to King David. They vary only after King David. In tracing Jesus' line back to Adam and God, for both Gospels (instead of Luke's only), two significant points are made evident, and that is that (1) Jesus had an ancient place in the race of men, and (2) as God's anointed deliverer, Jesus has significance for all of humanity and not just the Jews (KJV. *Text and annotation* 3:23-38, page 1492).

Because God called Abraham to be the ancestral progenitor of the chosen people of God—through whom his son, Jesus Christ, would take on human flesh to fulfill the Father's redemptive plan—we will consider the span from Abraham's birth in about 2165 B.C. (Hindson, 2013, *text and annotation* 11:26-32; pg.28) to the end of King David's reign in 1010–970 B.C. (Hindson, 2013, pg. 473; 1 Samuel 17:12) in Jerusalem. (David reigned for seven years over Judah in Hebron, until Ish-bosheth, Saul's son who became King in Israel, was defeated in about 1003 B.C. King David then moved to Jerusalem—formerly Urushalem, Salem. Melchizedek was King, as mentioned in Genesis 14:18—and made it the capital because of its central location between the northern tribes and the southern tribes; secondly, its topography makes it easy to defend. It was King David who gave it the name Jerusalem, which is often referred to as the "city of David" (Hindson, 2013, *Doctrinal footnote*, 5:5 pg. 503)

A period of about 1,196 years—from the birth of Abraham in 2165 B.C. to King David's end of the reign in Hebron in 1003 B.C. + 33 years reign in Jerusalem through 970 B.C. (Park, 2014, pg.156; that is 1163+33) is the first period presented in the Matthean genealogy of Jesus Christ. The second spans the time from the end of King David's reign in 970 B.C. to the deportation of Jeconiah/Jehoiachin to Babylon in 597 B.C.—a period

---

[4] Adam to Terah - Wikipedia, 2020 (Wikipedia, 2020), Sanctified – set apart or separate for God's purposes – because it could have gone through Esau or Reuben instead of through Jacob and Judah

of about 400 years. The third period of the genealogy of Jesus Christ spans from Jeconiah in 597 B.C. to the birth of Jesus Christ, the Messiah, around 4 or 5 B.C.—almost 593 years.

Regarding our main title, I'd like to draw our attention to what's said in Romans 8:28-30 (emphasis added):

> *And we know that all things work together for good to them that love God, to them who are the **called** according to his **purpose**.*

> *For whom he did **foreknow**, he also did **predestinate** to be conformed to the image of his Son, that he might be the **firstborn** among many brethren.*

> *Moreover, whom he did predestinate, them he also called: and whom he called, them he also **justified**: and whom he justified, them he also **glorified**.*

CHAPTER II

THE GARDEN OF EDEN

Adam and Eve

The first messianic prophecy in the Scripture **Protoevangelium**, that is, **First Gospel;** (Hindson, 2013, *Doctrinal footnote*, 3:15 pg.15) was made when the Lord said the **seed** of the woman shall crush or "shall bruise thy head, and thou shalt bruise his heel," that is, the serpent—or Satan's—heel (Genesis 3: 15). Scholars have long recognized this verse as the first Messianic prophesy of the Bible, thus the name **Protoevangelium**. It contains the first glimpse of the gospel, revealing three essential truths: {1} that Satan is the enemy of the human race, **"between thee"**—Satan—**and the woman**; {2} that he would place a spiritual barrier between **thy seed** (Satan's people) and **her seed** {God's people} and {3} that the representative of the woman (i.e., a human being; Christ) would deliver the death blow to Satan. He **shall bruise** {literary "crush"} **thy seed, and thou shalt bruise his heel** refers to Christ's bruising on the cross, which led to the eventual crushing of Satan and his Kingdom (Hindson, 2013, *text and annotation* 3:15, pg.14). The above analysis quoted from Hindson, *text and annotation* 3:15, page 14, supports the conclusion that the fulfillment of this messianic prophecy came in the incarnation and birth of Christ (Matthew 1: 25). "But when the fullness of time was come, God sent forth his Son made of woman, made under the law." [5]

The first couple was Adam, *Adamah,* literary means "ground" (the "Earthman," referring to mankind in general; Hindson, 2013, Note 2;20,

---

[5] Hindson, 2013, 3:15, p.15; also Galatians 4:4

pg.12) and Eve ("Mother of all living"; Hindson, 2013, 3:20, pg.15). They had several children (Genesis 5:4), but only three are mentioned in the Bible: Cain ("Acquire"), Abel ("Breath" or "Nothing"), and Seth ("In Adam's likeness," i.e., "Man; a sinful man").

Seth was born after Cain had killed Abel out of jealousy (when his first fruit offering was not accepted by God, but Abel's was seen in Genesis 4:4-10). Cain was cursed by God, so he left the Garden and became a vagabond (Genesis4:12).

God promised Adam, another son. He called him Seth, and Eve said, "For God . . . hath **appointed** me another seed instead of Abel, whom Cain slew" (Genesis 4:25, emphasis added). This indicates God's early planning stages in the human phase of the lineage of the coming of his Son. Seth has been "appointed" as the first individual in the human phase of the process in which each generation is recorded. The promise of chosen people (Jews) is kept through the call of Abraham and his seed until the birth of Jesus Christ, the Messiah.

Adam lived for 930 years (Genesis 5: 5). The only recorded descendant of Adam and Eve, Seth (son of their son Shem), became the first human to belong in the genealogy of the Messianic line of Jesus Christ, the Messiah, through the seed of a woman (Gen 3:15; 4:25; 5:1-5; 9:27).

Seth

Seth was the third son of Adam and Eve. He became the forefather of the godly line of their descendants. He was 105 years when Enos/Enosh was born to him and his wife, Aklia[i] (Craane, 1926, The lost books of the Bible and the forgotten books of Eden: Adam and Eve, page 65). Seth happened to be the ancestral father of the first human, Enoch (Genesis 5:24;), not to die, "...was translated that he should not see death, and was not found..." (Heb. 11:5) and the longest living man, Methuselah (Hindson, 2013, *Doctrinal footnote* 5:3, pg.18; cf. Hebrew (11:5)); as well as the ancestor of Noah who built the Ark and survived the great flood (Genesis5:29). Seth's considered by Jews to be "honored among men."[6]

The intermarriage between his godly line and the daughters of men— the ungodly line of his elder brother Cain—led to the judgment of the

---

[6] Hindson, 2013, Doctrinal footnote 5:3, pg. 18

Great Flood. Seth, who became the forefather of the godly line of the descendants of the sons of Adam (Hindson, 2013, pg. 18), had more sons and daughters, and the godly messianic line went through his son Enos (Genesis 5:7, 11). Seth lived for another 807 years after the birth of Enos and died at the age of 912, after commanding Enos to minister to his people faithfully, and not to associate with the children of Cain the murderer and sinner (The Lost Books, 1963), thus leaving Enos as his sole heir (Genesis 5:6-9). The line of Seth, "The Appointed," led to Noah, "The Deliverer."

Enos/Enosh

Enos and Noam, his wife (*Lumpkin, 2011*), had their first son, Cainan/ Kenan when he was ninety years old. He lived during the antediluvian period. Enos lived another 815 years after the birth of Cainan and was said to have more sons and daughters, but the godly seed of the messianic line went through Cainan, who was the only son mentioned. He lived during the antediluvian period was an uncle of Cain and Abel and a cousin to Enoch. He lived to be 905 before joining his ancestors (Genesis 5:11).

Cainan/Kenan

Cainan and his wife Muleleth (Book of Jubilees, 4:14-15;*Wikipedia, 2020*) had their first child when he was seventy years old. He named his son Mahalaleel/Maleleel. Cainan lived another 840 years after the birth of Mahalaleel and had more sons and daughters (Genesis 5:12-13; 1 Chronicles 1:2). Some claim that Cainan's father was Arphaxad (Luke 3:36) or that it may be a different Cainan; or maybe Luke got it mixed up with Canaan, the son of Ham, Noah's grandson. However, Arphaxad's father was Sem/Shem (one of Noah's sons and not Seth, the son of Adam, Genesis 10:21). It is possible that Luke 3:36 confused the names of the two patriarchs, Seth and Sem/Shem. Another observation is that Luke is the only Scripture writer to mention Arphaxad as Cainan's father. Such misidentification might occur because of gaps between the generations. Cainan lived for 910 years before joining his ancestors (Genesis 5:14).

Mahalaleel/Malelee

Mahalaleel was allegedly born around 3366 B.C. (Mahalaleel-Wikipedia, *en.m.wikipedia.org*) to Cainan and Muleleth, his mother. He and his wife Dinah, daughter of Barakiel (Book of Jubilees 4:14-15; *familypedia.wiki.org*), had their first child, Jared, when Mahalaleel was sixty-five years old (Genesis 5:15); and later had Danel (Mahalaleel—*ibid*). Mahalaleel's grandparents were Enos and Noam. Mahalaleel considered by some to be a Prophet who predicted the flood and warned his son about it before he died. Mahalaleel was the son who followed the godly prophetic lineage of Christ—even though Scripture says he had other sons and daughters----- he was the only one mentioned (Genesis 5:16). Mahalaleel lived another 830 years before dying at 895 years (2471B.C.)—enough time to have more children.

Jared

Jared was 162 years old when he and Baraka, his wife (Jared biblical figure, *en.m.wikipedia.org*), had their first child, whom he named Enoch. Jared had more sons and daughters (Genesis 5:18), but the messianic line went through his eldest son, Enoch. His name means "descend" because, in his days, it was said angels of the Lord descended to earth. He died when he was 962 (Genesis 5:20).

Enoch

Enoch was born during the antediluvian period in Babylon (Oxford, 1995) and was sixty-five years old when his son Methuselah was born; other children mentioned were Regim and Gaidad. [7] [8] Allegedly, he was born "birthmarked with a dot on the inner right arm, opposite the elbow." He is venerated by several Christian denominations, including the Armenian Catholic Church, Ethiopian Catholic Church, Roman Catholic Church,

---

[7] Crane, F. Dr. (1926), *The Lost Books of the Bible and the Forgotten Books of Eden*, pg.82.
[8] Lumpkin, J. B. (2009) *The Second Book of Enoch; The Slavonic Secrets of Enoch*, pg. 82, 1970

and the Oriental Orthodoxy, among many others. He is believed to have been the author of four books: "The First Book of Enoch; The second Book of Enoch-The Slavonic Secrets of Enoch; The third Book of Enoch— The Hebrew Book of Enoch. The Book of Fallen Angels, The Watchers, and the Origins of Evil" (Lumpkin, 2011, The Books of Enoch). Enoch was the first patriarch reported to have "walked with God," implying he had a good fellowship. The Epistle of Jude 1:14 referred to him as the "... seventh from Adam..." (Jude - Biblestudytools/dictionary; Oxford, 19). He was the first patriarch not to experience death: "And he was not, for God took him," in another word, "*he was raptured directly to heaven*" (Hindson, 2013, *Doctrinal footnote* 5:3, pg.18) or as Hebrew (11:5) states, "By faith, Enoch was translated that he should not see death; and he was not found, because God had translated him: for before his translation he had this testimony, that he pleased God." He was translated when he was 365 years old (Genesis 5:23-25). The same Hebrew word is used for the "*translation*" of Elijah in 2 Kings 2:3-5; he went to heaven without dying. This means he was raptured to heaven without dying. His bodily *translation*, according to observation in (Hindson 2013, *text and annotation* 5:21-24, pg. 19), was a sign that ultimately means reconciliation with God and includes a victory over death. Centuries later, the Prophet Elijah had the same divine experience (2 Kings 2:3-5).

Methuselah

Methuselah ("Man of the javelin" or "Death of Sword") lived during the antediluvian period and has the distinction of being the man who lived the longest in history—969 years (Genesis 5:21-27; Hindson, 2013, *K.J.V., Study Bible*, second edition, *Doctrinal footnote* 5:3, pg.18; Methuselah - Wikipedia, *en.m.wikipedia.org; cf.* Crane, *1926,* The lost books of the Bible; Adam and Eve, *page80-81*). Among his sons and daughters was Lamech, who was born when Methuselah was 187 years old. He lived another 782 years after the birth of Lamech—more than enough to produce more children before he died. It is believed that he died during the year of the Great Flood after the Ark was built, but he died before the actual flood (allegedly, God promised not to have him killed with the unrighteous). There is some today who believed he was a prophet. Both he and his son Lamech were the godly chosen by God to represent the messianic line (Luke 3:23-38).

Lamech

Lamech was 182 years old when Noah ("Rest") was born to him. He commented, "This same shall comfort us concerning our work and toil of our hands, because of the ground which the LORD hath cursed" (Genesis 5:29). Lamech lived another 595 years after having Noah and had more sons and daughters before his death at 777 (Genesis 5:30-31; Crane, 1926, *Ibid*). The genealogical line moves from the list of the righteous individuals who lived before the Great Flood to the sons of Noah.

Noah

Noah ("Rest") had three children—Shem, Ham, and Japheth—by the time he was five hundred years old (Genesis5:32). Japheth was the oldest and Ham the youngest, but Shem is always mentioned first because it was through him that God's Messiah would come. Noah was the last of the pre-Flood patriarchs. He was commissioned by God to build the Ark that survived the Great Flood. It is said he labored faithfully to build the Ark at God's command, ultimately saving not only his family but mankind and all land animals from extinction. He was six hundred years old when the Great Flood began, and he lived through it to be 950.

During Noah's generation, there was lots of wickedness; "And God saw that the wickedness of man was great in the earth... And it repented the Lord that he had made man on the earth, and it grieved him at his heart..." (Genesis6:5-7). Especially in the daughters of men, the ungodly line of Cain, and some of the sons of God, the godly line of Shem (Genesis 6:1-4). While the words "sons of God" refer to angels in some instances, they clearly don't here. Jesus taught that angels are not given in marriage (Matthew 22:29-30). Due to these spiritually mixed marriages, God brought judgment on the primeval world: "It repented the LORD that he had made man on earth, and it grieved him at his heart" (Genesis 6:6). This in no way means that God made mistakes in his dealing with men. Instead, it's a change in his divine direction as a result of man's behavior.

In all of this, Noah was said to have found "grace in the eyes of the LORD" by being just, righteous, and a man of obedience and faith who preached righteousness to his generation (Genesis 6:8). At the end of the Flood, "God blessed Noah and his sons, and said unto them, Be fruitful, multiply, and replenish the earth" (Genesis 9:1). God also made a covenant—the Noahic covenant—with Noah and his children, saying, "And I, Behold, I establish my covenant with you, and with your seed after you; And with every living creature that is with you... neither shall all flesh be cut off any more by the waters of a flood; neither shall there anymore be a flood to destroy the earth" (Genesis 9:9-11). The Noahic covenant allowed mankind the dispensation to govern itself on behalf of God. God sealed his covenant with Noah and his children by a sign of the rainbow (Genesis 9:12-17).

Under the Noahic Covenant, according to (Hindson 2013, *Doctrinal footnote* 9:12, Pg.24), man's relationship with the earth and to the order of nature was confirmed. God had promised never to use universal flood again to judge the world. Man's failure under this dispensation resulted in the building of the tower of Babel, which led to the judgment of the dispersion of tongues (Crane, 1926. Genesis11:1-3, 7).

Shem

As noted before (Hindson, 2013, *text and annotation* 9:18, pg.24), even though Sem/Shem (Luke 3:36) was not Noah's oldest son, he was the one in whom the messianic line flowed (Luke 3:23-38). At the end of the Flood, Noah got a bit careless with wine (Genesis9:21). Ham found him naked and told his other brothers. Shem and Japheth took a cloth and went backward to cover their father's nakedness. Noah then cursed Canaan, son of Ham, saying he would be a servant of servants to his brothers[9]. To Shem, he said, "Blessed be the LORD God Shem, and Canaan shall be his servant" (Genesis 9:26). To Canaan, he said, "Cursed be Canaan; a servant of servants shall he be unto his brethren" (Genesis 9:25). To Japheth, he said, "God shall enlarge Japheth, and he shall dwell in the tents of Shem, and Canaan shall be his servant" (Genesis 9:27).

---

[9] Wikipedia, 2020 (Wikipedia, 2020) "Ham's curse" did not affect all Ham's descendants   only the Canaanites.

Shem was chosen to represent the messianic line in part because of the blessing he received from his father. Shem had between five and nine children. One was Arphaxad, born when Shem was a hundred years. Others were (not in birth order) Elam, Aram, Asshur, Lud, Uz, Meshech/Mash, Hul, and Gether (Genesis 10:23; 1 Chronicles 1:17-18). Shem was the ancestor of the sematic peoples—including the Hebrews. His blessing says, "Blessed be the Lord God of Shem, and Canaan shall be his servant," a spiritual blessing by virtue of his knowing YHWH (Genesis9:26; Hindson, 2013, *text and annotation* 9:26, pg.25)—and one of eight people who survived the flood. Canaan became the father of the ancestor of the Canaanites in Canaan. He died at the age of 600.

Arphaxad

Arphaxad was born in Mesopotamia (modern Iraq) two years after the Great Flood, probably in c. 2325 B.C. (Arpachshad-Wikipedia, *en.m.wikipedia.org*), when his father, Shem, was a hundred years old. According to Genesis 11:12-13, he didn't have a child until he was thirty-five when he and his wife Rasu'aya (Jubilees 8) had Salah/Shelah. He lived another 403 years after having Salah (Genesis 11:12-13) and had more sons and daughters before he died at 438. Arphaxad belongs to one of the godly lines of the Messiah mentioned in Luke 3:23-38.

Salah/Shelah

Salah was thirty years when he and his wife, Mu'ak, had their first child, Eber/Heber. He lived another 403 years and had more sons and daughters before dying at 433 (Genesis 11:14-15).

Eber/Heber

Eber/Heber had two sons: Peleg (or Phalec/Phaleg) when he was thirty-four and Joktan later (Genesis11:16; Eber-Wikipedia, 2020). The name Eber is alleged to be the original eponym of the Hebrew people. Eber is the name mentioned in Luke 3:23-38 as one of the godly individuals in the lineage of Jesus Christ. According to Genesis 11:16-17, he lived another

430 years after the birth of his children and died at the age of 464, when Jacob was 20 years, c.1817 B.C. (Jacob-Wikipedia, 2020).

Peleg/Phalec

Peleg/Phalec ("division"), "so-called because in his days was the earth divided" (Easton's dictionary on *Biblestudytools*; Genesis 10:25), was thirty years old when he had Reu/Ragau. The meaning of his name notes he was born during the time of the "dispersion"—that is, the scattering of tongues at the Tower of Babel. Some have argued the name referred to the dispersion of the races which sprang from Eber, the one spreading towards Syria and Mesopotamia, and the other southward into Arabia (Easton's dictionary on *Biblestudytools.com*). The dispersion means that what men would not do willingly, God forces them to do it as the result of the judgment, and today we have more than three thousand languages and dialects. The positive effect of this confusion is the scattering of mankind (Hindson, 2013, 11:1-9, pg.27). In Israel, it's used as a surname. In English, it means "brook," a little river. Peleg lived up to 239 years and had more sons and daughters.

The considerable shortening of the life span from Eber to Peleg—from 464 to 239—might indicate that Eber may be a distant ancestor of Peleg.[10]

Reu/Ragau

Reu (means "his friend" or "his shepherd"; Hitchcocks Bible names dictionary on *Biblestudytools*) was thirty-two years old when Serug/Saruch was born to him. He lived another 207 years and died c.2213 B.C. (Smith's bible names dictionary at *Biblestudytools*) at the age of 239 (Genesis 11:20).

Serug/Saruch

Serug had Nahor when he was thirty years old. In the **Book** of **Jubilees,**[11] it is stated that his original name was Seroh. After Nahor

---

[10] Hindson, 2013, 10:25, pg. 26

[11] Book of Jubilees - Wikipedia, 2020 (Wikipedia, 2020): Considered Canonical by the Ethiopian Orthodox Church but not by the Protestant, Roman Catholic or the Eastern Orthodox Churches.

was born, Serug lived another 200 years, around c.2180 B.C. (Smith's Bible dictionary on *Biblestudytools*). He had more sons and daughters before he died at the city of Ur, Kesdim (Book of Jubilees - Wikipedia, *en.m.wikipedia.org*), at the age of 230 (Genesis 11:22-23).

Nahor

Nahor had Terah, Abraham's father, at the age of twenty-nine. He lived another 119 years and had more sons and daughters (Genesis11:25) before he died at the City of Ur at the age of 148 (Nahor son of Terah - Wikipedia, *en.m.wikipedia.org*). He was the grandfather of Abram/Abraham.

Thara/Terah

Terah had Abram[12], Nahor, and Haran. The name Terah means "wild goat, wanderer, loiterer" or "Higher Father." He was born Abram was not the oldest in the family, but he's always mentioned first because God chose him for the messianic line. Haran, the youngest, died after his first son, Lot, was born. Terah moved his family—Abram and his barren wife, Sarai[a]; Nahor and his wife, Milcah; the daughter of Haran; Lot; his father in law, father of Milcah and the father of Iscah—from Ur of the Chaldees to Haran in Canaan, and they dwelt there. Terah died in Ur of the Chaldees, Haran, at the age of 205 (Hindson, 2013, text and annotation 11:26-32, pg.28).

Abram/Abraham

Abram, as already referenced, was probably born around 2165 B.C.[13] The name Abram means "Exalted Father" or "Higher Father." This signifies his honored status as the progenitor of God's chosen people, the Hebrews. He had two other brothers, Nahor (the elder) and Haran (the youngest, who died early after the birth of his son Lot). Even though Abram was not the oldest, his name is always mentioned first in the Scripture because

---

[12] *Wikipedia, 2020* (Wikipedia, 2020), Later called Abraham and Sarah; Abraham's sister, same father different mothers.
[13] Hindson, 2013, text and annotation, 11:26-32, pg. 28

he was chosen by God for the Messianic line. Both Abram and Nahor got married in their native land of Ur of the Chaldees—Abram to Sarai (his half-sister) and Nahor to Milcah—before their father, Terah, moved the whole family to Haran[14] in Syria (Genesis 11:28-30), and died at the age of 205, Genesis 11:32.

From Haran, God called Abram and said:

> *Get thee out of thy country, and from thy kindred, and from thy father's house, unto a land, I will shew thee: And I will make thee a great nation, and I will bless thee, and make thy name great; and thou shalt be a blessing: And I will bless them that bless thee, and curse him that curseth thee: and in thee shall all the families of the earth be blessed* (Genesis 12:1-3)

Abram then moved to Canaan with Sarai, his wife, and Lot, his nephew, to Sichem-Shechem, a land where God promised him that his descendants would ultimately dwell (Genesis15:1-6).

Genesis 12:10-20 tells us how he moved to Egypt due to famine in the land. While in Egypt, out of fear that Abram might be killed because of Sarai's beauty, the two devised a scheme to say that she was his sister. He was very insightful in his assessment. As soon as they arrived, the Pharaoh was informed of Sarai's beauty. Upon being told she was Abram's sister, he immediately married her. The Pharaoh compensated Abram with sheep, oxen, asses, camels, and servants. But God was displeased. Plagues befell the house of the Pharaoh, and God instructed him in a dream to immediately return Sarai to Abram. After questioning Abram about the lie, the Pharaoh sent him away.

Abram returned to Canaan and, eventually, journeyed to Beth-el (Genesis 13:1-3). From there, he parted ways with Lot (he had a large herd). Everywhere Abram went, he was not truthful about his relationship with Sarai. For instance, he left Egypt and moved to Gerar, where he

---

[14] Nahor son of Terah" (Wikipedia, 2020) Wikipedia, 2020, A commercial center probably founded by the Sumerians from Ur, which became the Babylonians' moon cult hub.

told Abimelech, the King, that Sarai was his sister. Like the Pharaoh, Abimelech had Sarai brought to him as a wife.

Once more, God became angry and appeared to Abimelech in a dream, saying, "Thou art but a dead man, for the woman which thou hast taken, for she is a man's wife" (Genesis 20:3). Abimelech tried to argue his case by claiming ignorance, and God answered by saying; "Yea, I know that thou didst this in the integrity of thy heart; for I also withheld thee from sinning against me: therefore, suffered I thee not to touch her" (Genesis 20:5-6). God, therefore, advised Abimelech to "restore the man his wife; for he is a prophet, and he shall pray for thee, and thou shalt live: and if thou restore her not, know thou that thou shalt surely die, thou, and all that are thine" (Genesis 20:7). In the morning, Abimelech called Abraham and questioned him about the lie. He restored Sarai to Abraham with generous gifts in sheep, oxen, menservants, and maids. He instructed him to settle anywhere he chose within his Kingdom in peace (Genesis 20:8-15). Thus, "God's sovereignty overcame Abram's sin."[15]

Sarai was barren, so she advised Abram to try and get a child with her handmaid, Hagar, an Egyptian (Genesis 16:1-4). Shortly after, Hagar had a child and called his name Ismail ("God hears"). When Abram was ninety-nine years old, God renewed his covenant, saying:

> *I am the Almighty God; walk before me, and be thou perfect. And I will make my covenant between me and thee, and will multiply the exceedingly... Behold, my covenant is with thee, and thou shalt be a father of many nations. Neither shall thy name any more be called Abram, but thy name shall be Abraham; for a father of many nations have I made thee. And I will make thee... fruitful... And I will give unto thee, and to thy seed after thee, the land ... for an everlasting possession... Every man child among you shall be circumcised... And he that is eight days old shall be circumcised among you (Genesis 17"1-2, 4-6, 8, 10, 12).*

God further told Abraham that, as for his wife, "thou shalt not call her name Sarai, but Sarah shall her name be" (Genesis 17:15). The Lord God

---

[15] Hindson, 2013, 12:11-20, pg. 31.

also said to Abraham, "Sarah thy wife shall bear thee a son indeed, and thou shalt call his name Isaac: and I will establish my covenant with him for an everlasting covenant, and with his seed after him" (Genesis 17:19). When Abraham heard this, he "fell upon his face, and laughed, and said in his heart, Shall a child be born unto him that is a hundred years old? and shall Sarah, that is ninety years old, bear?" (Genesis 17:17).

Sarah's reaction was similar to that of her husband when she heard it: "Sarah laughed within herself, saying After I am waxed old shall I have pleasure, my lord being old also?" (Genesis 18:12). But the Lord said to Abraham, "And the LORD said unto Abraham, wherefore did Sarah laugh, saying, Shall I of a surety bear a child, which am old? Is anything too hard for the LORD? At the time appointed, I will return unto thee, according to the time of life, and Sarah shall have a son. Then Sarah denied, saying, I laughed not; for she was afraid. And he said, Nay; but thou didst laugh" (Genesis 18:13-15).

At about the exact time the Lord God had promised Abraham and Sarah, she conceived and bore Abraham a son in his old age (Genesis21:1-7), and he called him Isaac ("Laughter"); and Sarah gave God praise. Abraham circumcised his eight-days-old son as the Lord had commanded him. Isaac then became the carrier of the everlasting covenant (Genesis 21:12; Crane, 1926. Genesis17:19).

After the death of Sarah at the age of 127, at Kirjath-Arba (Genesis23:1), an old name for Hebron---which means "City of Four" (Crane, 1926. Josh. 14:15; Judg. 1:10); Abraham married Keturah and had five children with her (Genesis 25:1-6). But, like Hagar, she's classed as his concubine (Genesis 25:6). Just like with Ismael, Abraham gave unto Keturah's children "gifts, and sent them away from Isaac, his son, while he yet lived, eastward, unto the east country" (Genesis 25: 6). Abraham lived to be 175 years old (Genesis25:7-11).

In the Bible, he has portrayed "as the father of faith in God because of his faithful obedience to God's call and subsequent commands. His greatest test came in his obedience regarding Isaac at Mount Moriah" (Hindson, 2013, *Doctrinal footnote* 12:1; pg.29). The New Testament regards him as the ancestral father of Israel (Acts. 13:26).

Isaac

Isaac represented the ancestral line of the promised Messiah. God tested Abraham's faith by commanding him to sacrifice his only son, Isaac, at Mount Moriah (Genesis22:1-3). Isaac's obedience certainly anticipated—or foretold—Christ as the only begotten son willing to be bound on the Altar of sacrifice by his father[16].

Isaac's marriage to Rebekah was a demonstration of the Biblical balance of divine sovereignty {God's choice} and human responsibility {human choice}; (Hindson, 2013, *Doctrinal footnote* 24:13-67, pg.50). This is clearly shown in the oath Abraham's servant took and in his prayer near the well, asking for the correct girl and her willingness to travel with him back to Canaan (Genesis 24:1-9). When Rebekah came to the well and responded in compliance with the servant's prayer, he worshipped the Lord. Upon hearing the servant's tale, Laban (her brother) and Bethuel (her father and son of Nahor, brother to Abraham, Genesis 24:15) replied, "The thing proceedeth from the LORD:

We cannot speak unto thee bad or good" (Genesis 24:50). When Rebekah was asked if she would be willing to travel back to Canaan with Abraham's servant, she immediately agreed—to her family's surprise.

Abraham's faith was tested for twenty years as he waited for the birth of Isaac's sons, Jacob and Esau (Hindson, 2013, *Doctrinal footnote*, 21:3, pg.44). It is said the boys were born when Isaac was sixty years old (Genesis 25:26). Isaac, like his father, lied about his wife being his sister at Gerar: "And the men of the place asked him of his wife; and he said, She is my sister: for he feared to say, She is my wife; lest, said he, the men of the place should kill me for Rebekah; because she was fair to look upon" (Genesis 26:6-7). Isaac lived 180 years and had only those twins, Esau and Jacob (Hindson, 2013, *ibid* 21:3, pg.44; Crane, 1926; Genesis 35:28-29).

Jacob

Jacob was born clutching the heel of his twin brother, Esau, who was born first (Genesis 25:25-26). Jacob obtained Esau's birthright by taking advantage of his hunger as a hunter (Genesis 25:31-33). Jacob also deceived

---

[16] Hindson (2013), *K.J.V., Study Bible*, 2nd Edition, *Doctrinal Footnote* 12:3, pg. 44

his father, Isaac, into giving him Esau's blessings (a tradition that often goes to the eldest son). Jacob was able to accomplish the feat by conniving with Rebekah, his mother (Genesis 27:1-29). This act of betrayal (Hindson, 2013, Doctrinal footnote, 25:25, pg;53) led to animosity between the brothers (and, later, their descendants), forcing Jacob to flee for his life to Haran, where he eventually married Rachael and Leah (Genesis 29:21-29), the daughters of Laban (his mother's brother), and became the father of the twelve tribes of Israel—including the children born of their handmaids, Bilha (Rachael's) and Zilpah (Leah's, Genesis 29:1-35; 30:1-24; 35:16-20). Jacob's prosperity caused a deep divide between him and his uncle. Laban became openly hostile after a long period of simmering anger (31:1-7) because Jacob had used selective breeding (in addition to divine help) to prosper (Genesis 31:10-12). It was at this point that God appeared to Jacob and told him to return to Canaan: "Return unto the land of thy fathers, and to thy kindred, and I will be with thee" (Genesis 31:3).

Laban became openly hostile and angry (Genesis 25:5-7) when Jacob told him he needed to return (even though his wives supported him), saying, "Now then, whatsoever God hath said unto thee, do" (Genesis 31:16).

Jacob's name was changed to "Israel" after he wrestled with an angel of the Lord at Jabbok (Genesis 32: 22-32). Jacob returned to Canaan (Genesis 33:17-20) and stayed in Shechem for a while before eventually settling at Hebron. In his old age, he moved what was left of his family of seventy[17] (Rachael, as Genesis 35:16-20 tells us, had died when giving birth to her second son, Benjamin, between Beth-el and a little distance to Ephrath; she was buried at Ephrath, which is Bethlehem) to Egypt at the invitation of his son, Joseph, when the famine worsened in the land of Canaan. He died in Egypt at the age of 130 years (Hindson, 2013, *Doctrinal footnote* 25:26, pg. 53). He was buried in the cave of Machpelah, Hebron (a cave Abraham had bought with the field of Ephron the Hittite "for a possession of a burying place," Genesis 49: 29-32; Crane, 1926. Hindson, 2013, *text and annotation*, 49:28-33, pg.94) with pomp and Pharaoh's full blessing and support.

---

[17] Park, gave a date of 1876 B.C. for Jacob's journey to Egypt without sufficient evidence or explanation, pg. 51.

Judah/Yahuda

Judah was the fourth son of Jacob and Leah (Genesis 50; Table of Sons of Jacob, pg. 96). He was born about 1566 B.C. (Judah - Wikipedia, 2020) in Mesopotamia (Paddan Aram), modern Iraq. He was said to die either in 1448 B.C. or 1447 B.C. (Judah - Wikipedia, 2020). Judah was the son that rose to a position of power amongst his brothers after he interceded to save the life of his brother Joseph when, because of jealousy, his other brothers had planned to kill him: "Judah said unto his brethren, what profit is it if we slay our brother, and conceal his blood? Come, and let us sell him to the Ishmeelites, and let not our hand be upon him; for he is our brother and our flesh. And his brethren were content" (Genesis 37: 26-27).

Genesis 38:1-10 tells us that Judah married a Canaanite called Shuah, "And Judah saw there a daughter of a certain Canaanite, whose name was Shuah[18]; and he took her, and went in unto her" (Genesis 38:2) and they had three children, Er, Onan, and Shelah. Er married a Canaanite called Tamar/Thamar, but he was found to be wicked in the sight of the Lord, and the Lord slew him (Gen. 38:7). Then Judah asked Onan, his son, to marry Tamar, his brother's wife, so he could "raise up seed" for him (verse 8), through the law of levirate. Onan knew the seed wouldn't be his, so when he went into his brother's wife, "he spilled it on the ground, lest that he should give seed to his brother" (verse 9). This act displeased the Lord, and he slew Onan (v.10).

In Jacob's blessings to his sons, Judah and his descendants were set to be in the Messianic line. Jacob, their father, blessed him and said,

> *Thy hand shall be in the neck of thine enemies... Judah is a lion's whelp... The sceptre shall not depart from Judah, nor a lawgiver from between his feet, until Shiloh come; and unto him shall the gathering of the people be. Binding his foal unto the* vine, *and his ass's colt unto the choice vine; he washed his garments in wine, and his clothes in the blood of grapes: His eyes shall be red with wine, and his teeth white with milk.* Genesis49: 8-12

---

[18] "Shuah" Wikipedia, 2020 (Wikipedia, 2020), Genesis 38:2, Hebrew shua

The reference to the sceptre was a symbol of power, and lawgiver refers to a mace (when a King or a dignitary was seated, his office's staff was held between his feet). The phrase "and unto him shall the gathering of the people be" means unto him shall be the obedience of all the people (Hindson, 2013, *text and annotation*, 49:1-27, pg.93). This statement has been interpreted by some scholars as referring to the Messiah (*ibid* above). Thus, the reference to the Lion in the blessing points to the one who is generally called "the Lion of the tribe of Judah" (Rev. 5:5).

Seeing that he had lost both adult sons, Judah said to his daughter-in-law, "Remain a widow at thy father's house, till Shelah my son be grown: for he said, Lest peradventure he also die, as his brethren did. And Tamar went and dwelt in her father's house" (Genesis 38:11). Meanwhile, Shuah, Judah's wife, died, and he took the time to mourn her. After the mourning, he went to see his sheepshearers at Timnath. Immediately, somebody informed Tamar that her father-in-law was on his way to visit his sheepshearers. Tamar had seen that Shelah had grown, and she hadn't been given to him as a wife. So, quickly, she removed her widow's garment and dressed, covering her head with a veil. She stood along the way that Judah had to pass through on his way to Timnath. When Judah saw her, he thought she was a "harlot" and said, "I pray thee, let me come in unto thee. . .. And she said, What wilt thou give me, that thou mayest come in unto me?" (Genesis 38:15-16). He said he would send her a "kid from the flock," and she insisted he give her a pledge to prove he would do it; he gave her his signet ring, bracelets, and the staff he was holding in his hand (Genesis 38:17-18).

Genesis 38:20-30 describes how, a few days later, he sent the kid from the flock with a friend to redeem the items he'd given as a pledge. The friend looked and asked everybody about a harlot, but they told him there had never been one there. A few months later, Judah was informed that his daughter had become pregnant through harlotry. He was fizzed and declared, "Bring her forth, and let her be burnt" (verse 24). When Tamar came, she said to her father-in-law, "By the man, whose these are, am I with child: and she said, Discern, I pray thee, whose are these, the signet, and bracelets, and staff" (verse 25). I presume Judah must have felt flabbergasted but acknowledged they were his, saying, "She hath been more righteous than I; because that I gave her not to Shelah my son"

(Genesis 38:26). Judah died between the ages of 108 or 109 in around 1448 B.C./1447 B.C. in Mesopotamia, modern Iraq, or Israel (Judah - Wikipedia, *en.m.wikipedia.org*).

Pharez/Perez/Phares

According to Genesis 38:27-30, Tamar had twins, Pharez/Perez and Zarah/Zerah. The miracle of the birth was that Zarah (the meaning in Hebrew is "dawning" or "shining") showed his hand first, and the midwife put a scarlet thread as a sign that he came out first; but then he withdrew, and Pharez zipped his way past him. The midwife was surprised and said, "How hast thou broken forth? This breach be upon thee: therefore, his name was called Pharez" (verse 29; his name means "breach" or "burst forth or out"). Pharez is listed in the genealogy of Christ in Matthew 1:3. The prenatal struggle mirrors that of Esau and Jacob (Genesis 38:27-29), and it brought a violent chapter to an end. These events launched the tribe of Judah on its career as the forefather of the gentle, righteous, and godly Joseph.00

The siblings of Pharez/Perez include Er, Onan, Shelah, and Zerah (Genesis 38:1-5; Genesis 46:12; Numbers 26:20-21). Pharez had two children, Hezron and Hamul, and three grandchildren through Hezron/ Esrom: Jerahmeel, Ram, and Chelubai (1 Chronicles 2:5-16). It is Esrom that is mentioned in the New Testament in the lineage of the Messiah in Luke 3:23-38.

Ram/Aram

Ram was the first son of Hezron/Esrom and King David's ancestor (1 Chronicles 2:9-15; Ruth 4:19). In the New Testament, he's referred to as Aram or Arni (Crane, 1926. *Wikipedia, en.m.wikipedia.org*; Luke 3:23-38). Ram's first son was Amminadab (Ruth 4:19).

Amminadab

Amminadab was born in Egypt and had Nahshon/Naasson and ancestor of King David, and therefore the ancestor of Jesus Christ (Amminadab-Wikipedia, *en.m.wikipedia.org*). His daughter Elisheva was

Aaron's wife (Exodus 6:23), making him Aaron, Moses' brother, and the high priest's father-in-law. His grandchildren were Elisheba and Eleazar.

Nahshon/Naasson

Nahshon was born in Egypt (Nahshon – Wikipedia, *en.m.wikipedia.org*), and a brother-in-law of Aaron, the high priest, and Moses' elder brother (Aaron-Wikipedia, *en.m.wikipedia.org*). He later led the army or host of Judah as captain (Numbers 2:3). He was one of the heads of the tribes of Judah in the first census Moses conducted in the wilderness as instructed by God, as well as a leader in the offerings by the tribal princes as a representation of the tribe of Judah (Numbers 1:7; 2:3; 7:12, 17; 10:14). He was a brother-in-law of Aaron (*ibid*). According to the New Testament, he was also the father-in-law of Rahab. And according to the Jewish Midrash, he also initiated the Hebrew's passage through the Red Sea by walking in head-deep until the sea parted (*ibid*). One of Nahshon's sons mentioned in the lineage of Christ is Salma. Nahshon's great-grandchildren were Eleazar, Salmon, Phinehas, Elimelech, Abihu, and Nadab.

Salmon/Salma

Salmon/Salma is mentioned in Luke 3:23-38 and Matthew 1:4 as one of the sons of Nahshon and a person in the Messianic lineage. He was one of two spies whom Joshua sent to Jericho before he crossed the Jordon and attached it (Salmon {biblical figure}; *Wikipedia, 2020*); thus, becoming a member of the first generation of Israelites to cross the Jordan River (*ibid*). According to Scripture, Salmon eventually married (Salmon {bible}; *Wikipedia, en.m.wikipedia.org*) Rahab (the Canaanite harlot that hid the spies sent by Joshua to spy secretly on Jericho in Joshua 2:1-21, around 1407 B.C.; Hindson, 2013, *Doctrinal footnote*, 2:1, pg.353) and had Booz/Boaz, a son mentioned in Messianic lineage.

Boaz/Booz

Boaz/Booz ("in him is strength" or "in the strength of"; (Boaz-Wikipedia, 2020) married Ruth, the Moabite daughter-in-law of Naomi.

Boaz and Ruth had Obed, who later became Jesse's father, making Boaz the grandfather of Jesse, father to David, the Great King of both Judah and Israel. Thus, a Canaanite harlot and a Moabite woman became part of King David's lineage, from whom the Messiah descended (Ruth 4:20-22; Matthew 1:4-5; Luke 3:31-32).

Obed/Ohed

Obed ("worshipper"; (Obed {biblical figure}: *Wikipedia, en.m.wikipedia.org*) is a grandfather of David, hence named as one of Jesus' ancestors in the genealogies recorded in the Gospels of Matthew (Matthew 1:5) and of (Luke 3:32).

Jesse/Yishai/Isai

Jesse (in Hebrew, it means "King," "God exists," or "God's gift") was a successful farmer and a sheep breeder who lived in Bethlehem. Jesse had nine children, two of whom were girls, Zeruiah and Abigail; his firstborn son was Eliab, who was followed by Abinadab, Shimma, Nethaneel, Raddai, Ozem, and David (1 Chronicles 2:13-16). Abigail (the daughter of Nahash, the sister of Zeruiah), gave birth to Amasa, Absalom's commander (2 Sam.17:25; Crane, 1926. Hindson, 2013 2:16,17, pg.643). Zeruiah's son Joab became David's commander and strong supporter to the end. Even though David was the seventh and youngest, born in c. 1040 B.C., he was always listed first because he was the one chosen by God to lead the lineage of the Messiah.

CHAPTER III

PRE-EXILIC

Kings of Israel and Judah after Saul, most of whom formed part
of the genealogy of Jesus Christ according to Matthew 1:1-16

King David

David was the youngest son of Jesse of the tribe of Judah (1 Sam.16:11-12).
He was born around c.1040 B.C. and worked as a farmer with a large herd
of sheep. He was the second King of Israel at the age of thirty (2 Sam.5:4)
in 1040 B.C. (Hindson, 2013, *Doctrinal footnote*, 17:12, pg.473)—and the
most decorated of all the King He ruled for forty years, and his dynasty
ruled over Judah for over four hundred years.

David was blessed with children. Some were born when he was in
Hebron: his firstborn, with Ahinoam the Jezreelitess, was Ammon; his
second, Daniel/Chileab, was the son of Abigail, the Carmelitess[19] (1
Chronicles 3:1). With Maachah (daughter of Talmai, King of Geshur),
he had Absalom, and with Haggith, he had Adonijah (1 Chronicles 3:2).
With Abital, he had Shephatiah, and with Eglah, he had Ithream (1
Chronicles 3:3). Sons born to him in Jerusalem were Shimea/Shammua,
Shobab, Nathan, and Solomon (with Bath-shua/Bathsheba) and Ibhar,
Elishama/Elishua, Eliphelet/Elpalet, Nogah, Nepheg, Japhia, Elishama,

---

[19] Nabal, Wikipedia, 2020 (Wikipedia, 2020), Former wife of Nabal, who died
shortly after she told him she had seen David privately and convinced him not to
attack Nabal for his refusal to assist David and his men in the wilderness as a refuge.
David married her soon after (1 Samuel 25:2-42).

Eliada/Beeliada, and Eliphelet (1 Chronicles 3:5-8). These were a total of nineteen sons "beside the sons of the concubines, and Tamar their sister" (1 Chronicles 3:9).

In Scripture, he is shown to be an ancestor of Jesus (Matthew 1:1). He began his career as a shepherd boy (1 Sam.16:11; Hindson, 2013, *Ibid*, 17:12, pg.473) who demonstrated his prowess, courage, and faithfulness by killing lions and a bear who came to attack his sheep. He also played the harp in King Saul's court and (1 Sam.16:23), and subsequently, became a highly respected nobleman in King Saul's attendant after he slays Goliath, the Philistine. David became a national hero when he slaughtered the Philistines' giant, Goliath, using only a sling and a stone. Due to his popularity, animosity developed between David and Saul, so David became a fugitive. However, after Saul's death, the tribe of Judah elected David King of Judah (he was thirty years old), placing him on the throne in Hebron, where he ruled for seven years and six months.

After Saul's death, Abner—Saul's commander—appointed his son Ish-bosheth King over Israel (2 Samuel 2:8-11). However, after a few years of scuffles, King David of Judah defeated Israel; he was made King of the United Kingdom of Israel after a brief interlude. He ruled for thirty-three years in a city he named Jerusalem (2 Samuel 5:5). He built a palace in the highest section of the town (1 Chronicles 11:8), often referred to as Mount Zion. He also moved the Ark of the Covenant from Kirthjath-Jearim to Jerusalem (1 Chronicles 13:5-8; 1 Chronicles 15:15-29), where his son Solomon would build the temple David had dreamt of (2 Chronicles 3:1-2).

Like the Abrahamic covenant in Genesis 17 and the New Covenant in Jeremiah 31:31-37, the Davidic covenant constitutes an unconditional promise of God. The most important part of the covenant is that it will be an everlasting one. Thus, even though Israel would be taken into exile because of their disobedience and worship of other gods, God would regather them into the land so that, ultimately, God's promise to Israel will be fulfilled in the universal rule of the Messiah.

Solomon was the son David had with Bathsheba. 2 Samuel 11:2-4 tells us:

> *David arose from off his bed, and walked upon the roof of the Kings's house: and from the roof, he saw a woman washing*

herself; and the woman was very beautiful to look upon. And David sent and enquired after the woman. And one said, Is not this Bathsheba, the daughter of Eliam, the wife of Uriah the Hittite? And David sent messengers and took her, and she came in unto him, and he lay with her.

Following the encounter, Bathsheba became pregnant; and she said to King David, "I am with child" (2 Samuel 11:5). Eventually, David sent a letter to his commander, Joab, through Uriah, saying, "Set ye Uriah in the forefront of the hottest battle, and retire ye from him, that he may be smitten, and die" (2 Samuel 11:14-15). The irony of it all was that Uriah carried out his own death sentence.

After Uriah died, King David married Bathsheba; but God wasn't happy with David, so the child died after birth (2 Samuel 11:26-27; 12:19). God sent Prophet Nathan to King David to warn him, saying, "The sword shall never depart from thine house; because thou hast despised me, and hast taken the wife of Uriah the Hittite to be thy wife. Thus saith the Lord, Behold, I will raise up evil against thee out of thine own house, and I will take thy wives before thine eyes, and give them unto thy neighbor, and he shall lie with thy wives in the sight of this sun" (2 Samuel 12:1, 10-12).

Psalm 51 records David's repentance before God for what he did. Still, as a result of his sin, many things happened to him before his death. For instance, Absalom's attempted coup (2 Sam.15:7-12). He made efforts to overthrow him after openly abusing the King's concubines (2Sam.16:21-22) on the roof of the palace when David ran from the palace, leaving behind ten "concubines" (2 Sam.15:13-17; Hindson, 2013, *Doctrinal footnote*, 14:1, pg. 517) Ahithophel, once King David's counselor, broke ranks and stayed with Absalom, advising him, "Go in unto thy father's concubines, which he hath left to keep the house; and all Israel shall hear that thou art abhorred of thy father: then shall the hands of all that are with thee be strong" (2 Samuel 16:21-23).

Eventually, Joab killed Absalom at the Battle of Woods of Ephraim. After being informed of how Absalom's hair got caught in the boughs of a great oak, he said, "I may not tarry thus with thee. And he took three darts in his hand, and thrust them through the heart of Absalom"—even though the King had said before, "Deal gently for my sake with the young man, even with Absalom" (2 Samuel 18:5-14). Upon being told of Absalom's demise, the King cried, "O my son Absalom, my son, my son Absalom! would God I had died for thee, O Absalom, my son, my son!" (2 Samuel 18:31-33). King David mourned his son as he also mourned King Saul and Jonathan, Saul's son and David's best friend and protector (2 Sam.1:11-12; vs.17).

A few years after the Absalom debacle, King David was growing old—and becoming unpopular with the public, so Adonijah, his son with Haggith, struck by launching a coup (1 Kings 1:1-9). Seeing that those older than him among the sons of David had suffered violent deaths[20], Adonijah reasoned he had a legitimate right (1 Kings 1:5) to the throne—even though he knew the Lord had selected Solomon, and King David had said as much in private.

Aside from the curse God placed upon David for sinning with Bathsheba, King David had failed to discipline his sons properly (1 Kings 1:6). So Adonijah began his plot, gaining valuable allies in Joab, King David's Captain of the Host[21], and Abiathar the Priest. His next strategy was to hold some sort of a feast with his supporters, during which he would declare himself King (1 Kings 1:7-9). But Nathan the Prophet and Zadok the Priest had learned of Adonijah's claim to claim the throne.

Nathan approached Bathsheba (1 Kings 1:11), and asked her to go to the King and try to convince him to issue a public proclamation that would declare Solomon was the heir apparent (1 King 1:11-13). King David immediately appointed Zadok and Nathan and Benaiah his Chief of Staff in Spiritual and civil realms to arrange for Solomon to ride upon his personal mule and wear his personal apparel to Gihon, where he would be anointed publicly as King (1Kings 1:32-40).

The noise of the great pomp and fanfare carried over the hill to Adonijah and his supporters' party at En-rogel (1 King 1:41-46).[22] When

---

[20] Ammon at the hand of Absalom after he defiled his sister, Chileab/Daniel probably in early childhood, and Absalom at the hand of Joab at the Battle of Wood of Ephraim.

[21] "Joab" Wikipedia, 2020 (Wikipedia, 2020).

[22] "Solomon" Wikipedia, 2020 (Wikipedia, 2020), The news of Solomon's Kingship brought an abrupt end to Adonijah's plans. He sought mercy from Solomon by laying hold on the horns of the alter, a time- honored place of refuge for those who have committed unintentional crimes. He received a temporary relief but later killed.

Adonijah asked what the noise was about, Jonathan, son of Abiathar, said, "Verily our lord King David hath made Solomon King" (1 Kings 1:42-43). Eventually, King Solomon had Adonijah put to death, and he banished Joab and Abiathar (1 King 1:26-35; 2:22-25).

King David died peacefully in c. 970 B.C. (King David-Ancient; *ancient.eu;* Hindson 2013, *Doctrinal footnote*, 17:12, page 473) after a most successful time as King in Israeli history; and was buried in Jerusalem. David's charge to his son Solomon can be found in 1 Kings 2:2-9). Many have called his reign "The Golden Age" of the monarchy.

King Solomon

Solomon was the youngest son of King David and Bathsheba/Bath-Shua (1 Chronicles 3:5). He was born in about 990 B.C. in Jerusalem, Judah (Solomon-Wikipedia, *en.m.wikipedia.org*). He was blessed by Prophet Nathan, with the name Jedidiah (Hindson, 2013 *text and annotation,* 12:24, 25; pg.514). He was known as a wealthy and wise King of the united monarchy of Israel and Judah. As co-regent with his father, he was given some valuable advice regarding how to rule. He was the third and last King of united Israel. He reigned about forty years, from about 970 to 931 B.C. He was also known as Jedidiah ("Beloved of the Lord"; *ibid* or "Yahweh's Beloved"; 2 Samuel 12:25).

King Solomon, with whom the Davidic covenant is confirmed, became the son through whom the Messianic line continued (Hindson, 2013, *Doctrinal footnote*, 7:12-16, pg.507; Crane, 1926.2 Sam, 7:12-16, 29). He extended his father's geographical territory and the Monarchy's material wealth to their utmost. In later years, he lost his spiritual discernment due to his insatiable love for foreign women: "For it came to pass, when Solomon was old, that his wives turned away his heart after other gods: and his heart was not perfect with the LORD his God, as was the heart of David, his father." (1 King 11:1-4).

Due to political convenience and sensual living, he succumbed to apostasy, for which God chastised him (1 King 11:5-13). His political policies of oppression and desire for luxury almost led to the dissolution of the united monarchy (1 Kings 11:1-28; Hindson, 2013, *Doctrinal footnote*, 1:10, pg.540) which happened during the reign of his son Jehoboam, son of

Naamah, Pharaoh's daughter (1 King 12). Jehoboam wasn't the only son of King Solomon; there were others, like Menelik I, Taphath, and Basemath. But Jehoboam is the one always listed because he was the one chosen for the Davidic Messianic line.

King Solomon was well known for building the Temple and a magnificent palace (1 Kings 6–7). He also wrote Ecclesiastes, Song of Solomon, Psalm 72 and 127, and more than one thousand songs (Hindson, 2013, *Ibid*, 1:10, pg.540).

King Solomon had 700 wives, princesses, and 300 hundred concubines. King Solomon died at the age of 58/59 in c. 932/931 B.C. Solomon, with whom the Davidic line is confirmed, becomes the son through whom the Messianic line is continued. The names of his descendants in both pre- and post-Exile is listed in 1Chronicles 3:10-24. Verses 10-16 were names of pre-exilic descendants, and 17-24 were post-exilic.

Rehoboam

Rehoboam was the son of Solomon and Naamah, the Ammonitess (2 Chronicles 12:13; 1 Kings 14:21; Easton: *Biblestudytools*) and was born in c. 972 B.C. (Rehoboam-Wikipedia, 2020) in Jerusalem, Judah. He was forty-one years old when he began his reign with an impending challenge from Jeroboam, the son of Nebat, who had taken refuge in Egypt out of fear of King Solomon—but was immediately recalled by his supporters after King Solomon's death (1 Kings 12:1-1). Upon Jeroboam's return, all ten tribes of Israel sent a congregation to King Rehoboam saying, "Thy father made our yoke grievous: now, therefore, make thou the grievous service of thy father, and his heavy yoke which he put upon us, lighter, and we will serve thee" (1 King 12:4).

Rehoboam first consulted with the older men that had served his father, King Solomon, and they advised him to listen and agree with the demand of the people (1 King 12:6-7). But when he asked the opinion of the young men, they advised him:

> *Thus shalt thou speak unto this person that spake unto thee,*
> *saying, Thy father made our yoke heavy, but make thou it*
> *lighter unto us; thus shalt thou say unto them, My little finger*

> *shall be thicker than my father's loins. And now, whereas my*
> *father did lade you with a heavy yoke, I will add to your yoke:*
> *my father hath chastised you with whips, but I will chastise*
> *you with scorpions (*1 King 12:8-11).

With this response, the northern tribes rebelled against King Rehoboam. The people said to him,

> *What portion have we in David? Neither have we inheritance*
> *in the son of Jesse: to your tents, O Israel: now see to thine*
> *own house, David. So Israel departed unto their tents. But*
> *as for the children of Israel which dwelt in the cities of Judah,*
> *Rehoboam reigned over them* (1 King 12:16-19).

Jeroboam, son of Nebat, was then made King of the ten tribes in the North (1 Kings 12:20). The capital later moved to Samaria, after it was newly constructed under King Omri, where it remained until its fall in 722 B.C. (Hindson, 2013, *text and annotation*, 16:24; pg.575; 1 Kings 16:24).

Jehoboam had three wives who are mentioned: Mahalath the daughter of Jerimoth, the son of David; Michaiah/Maachah, daughter of Uriel of Gibeah and Tamar, Absalom's granddaughter; and Abihail, daughter of Eliab, son of Jesse (2 Samuel 14:27; 2 Chronicles 11:18-23). It is also mentioned that Maachah was Jehoboam's favorite out of the eighteen wives he had (2 Chronicles 11:21). His children with Michaiah were Abijah/Abia/Abijam, Attai, Ziza, and Shelomith (2 Chronicles 11:20). Those with Abihail were Jeush, Shamariah, and Zahan (2 Chronicles 11:18-19). In total, he is said to have had eighteen wives and threescore (thirty-six) concubines (2 Chronicles 11:21). He had twenty-eight sons and thirty-six daughters, but the Messianic line went to Abijah, Michaiah's son.

Rehoboam reigned for seventeen years in Jerusalem, Judah (2 Chronicles 12:13). Rehoboam did evil in the sight of the Lord by bringing back the worship of other gods and idols. Under his rule, cultic prostitution involving both sexes was also carried out at the Canaanite religious shrines. These debased practices contributed to God's judgment of Judah (2 Chronicles 12:1-2). However, his later repentance saved Jerusalem and Judah from total annihilation from Shishak, the King of Egypt (2

Chronicles 12:6-12). Rehoboam died around c. 913/915 B.C. in Jerusalem (Rehoboam-Wikipedia, 2020; *Wikipedia, en.m.wikipedia.org*).

Abijah/Abia/Abijam

Abijah was born in Jerusalem. In Hebrew, his name is Abiyyahu or Abiyyah, which means, "**Yahweh is my Father.**" It is stated, "And Rehoboam made Abijah the son of Maachah the chief, to be ruler among his brethren: for he thought to make him King" (2 Chronicles 11:22; 13:2).

He was, therefore, the fourth King of Judah; Abijah of Judah; *familypedia.Wikipedia, 2020.org*) of the house of David and the second of the Kingdom of Judah (2 Chronicles 13:1). Abijah "walked in all the sins of his father . . . and his heart was not perfect with the Lord his God, as the heart of David his father (1 King 15: 3). Despite his spiritual shortcomings, "for David's sake did the Lord his God give him a lamp in Jerusalem, to set up his son after him, and to establish Jerusalem" (1 King 15:4). During his reign, he endeavored to recover or bring back the ten tribes of the northern Kingdom of Israel and thereby made constant war with Jeroboam, the King of Israel. In one of the battles, of Mount Zemaraim, in Mount Ephraim, as narrated in 2 Chronicles 13:3-20, Abijah gave an uplifting godly speech to his men, leading to the slaughter of Israel (2 Chronicles 13:5-12); he "took cities from him, Bethel with the towns thereof, and Jeshanah with the towns thereof, and Ephraim with the towns thereof" (2 Chronicles 13:4-12, 19).

Abijah had fourteen wives, twenty-two sons, and sixteen daughters (Abijah of Judah/Familypedia/Fandom: *familypedia.wiki.org*). He reigned from about c. 913–911 B.C. or 915-913 B.C. and died in about 911/912 B.C.

Asa

Asa was the son of Abijah and Arsah (Asa of Judah-Wikipedia, *en.m.wikipedia.org*), and a grandson of Maachah, daughter of Abishalom (Hindson, 2013, *text and annotation*, 15:1-3, pg.572; 1 Kings 15:10). He was the third King of the Kingdom/Monarchy of Judah and the fifth of the house of David and reined for forty-one years in Jerusalem. He is said to have been born in Jerusalem in c.911 B.C.

Maachah, the mother of Abijam and grandmother of Asa, was a strong-willed person like a grandfather, and whose influence for evil was ended by Asa's reforms (Hindson, 2013, *ibid* 15:1-3; vv.9,10, pg.572; Crane, 1926. 2 Chronicles 15:16).

Asa did good in the eyes of the Lord (1 Kings 15:11-15) by removing the altars of the foreign gods, breaking down their images, and cutting down the "groves"[23] (2 Chronicles 14:2-3). He encouraged Judah to follow the Lord God of their fathers; thus, under him, there was peace in the Kingdom (2 Chronicles 14:4-5). He built fenced cities (2 Chronicles 14:6-15) and formed a large army of men of valor. He fought and defeated Ethiopia[24], and "they also smote the tents of cattle, carried away sheep and camels in abundance, and returned to Jerusalem" (2 Chronicles 14:15). Asa's early years were spent wisely, especially in regards to his spiritual, godly piety and his political purposes. In terms of reforms, even his grandmother, Maachah, saw the influence of her apostate religion dramatically annihilated (2 Chronicles 15:8-17).

Asa was threatened by Baasha, King of Israel, and he sought an alliance with Ben-Hadad, King of Syria (2 Chronicles 16:1-6). He sent Ben-Hadad, who at the time dwelt in Damascus, silver, and gold from the Temple—the house of God—and from the King's palace to help relieve him from the pressures put on his Northern frontier by Baasha. In response, Ben-hadad sent his captains and army against the cities of Israel, including all the store cities of Naphtali (2 Chronicles 16:1-4).

The Prophet Hanani was sent by the Lord God to rebuke King Asa of Judah. He said to him,

> *Because thou hast relied on the King of Syria, and not relied on the LORD thy God, therefore is the host of the King of Syria escaped out of thine hand. Were not the Ethiopians and the Lubims a huge host, with very many chariots and horsemen? Yet, because thou didst rely on the Lord, he delivered them into thine hand. For the eyes of the Lord run to and fro throughout the whole earth, to shew himself strong in the behalf of them whose heart is perfect toward him. Herein*

---

[23] Hindson (2013), Wooden images introduced in his father's reign.

[24] Hindson (2013), The Biblical Ethiopia refers to Cush, which is modern Sudan.

thou hast done foolishly: therefore from henceforth, thou shalt have wars. (2 Chronicles 16:7-9).

The Lord wasn't pleased with Asa for his breach of trust, especially of hiring the Aramean King to relieve the pressures put on his northern frontier by the Israelite Baasha (vv. 1-6), so, instead of saving him, he's rebuked by God's Prophet and judged him (2 Chronicles 16:9). Asa didn't take the message Prophet Hanani brought him from God Kindly, so he "put him in a prison house; for he was in a rage with him because of this thing. And Asa oppressed some of the people the same time." (2 Chronicles 16:10). This episode marked a turning point in Asa's spiritual decline.

Toward the end of his thirty-ninth-year reign (vv.12-14), he got an infection in his feet; it "was exceeding great: yet in his disease, he sought not to the LORD, but the physicians" (2 Chronicles 16:12). He reigned from c.911-869/870 B.C. and died two years into a coregency with his son Jehoshaphat, bringing his forty-one reign to an end in 869/870 B.C. (Asa of Judah- Wikipedia, *en.m.wikipedia.org*). According to Hindson (2013); **Outline of First Kings**, pg. 538-539; his son's reign is dated from 872-847 B.C. Asa was considered by his countrymen a righteous King. The Davidic line from here passed to his son with Azubah, Jehoshaphat.

Jehoshaphat/Josaphat

Jehoshaphat was the son of Asa with his wife Azubah (2 Chronicles 20:31; Asa of Judah- Wikipedia, 2020), daughter of Shilhi. He became King at the age of thirty-five, when his father died, around 870 B.C. (2 Chronicles 20:31; 1 King 15:24; 2 Chronicles 17:1) According to the Introduction to the First Book of Kings, pg.538-539, he reigned on his own, not as a co-regent from c.872-847 B.C. (Jehoshaphat: *britanica. com*). He was the fourth King of the Kingdom of Judah, in succession to his father. He reigned when Israel was reigned by Ahab, Ahaziah, and Jehoram. He kept close political and economic alliances with them (2 Chronicles 17:2-4) and set himself to cleanse the land of idolatry (1 Kings 22:43).

The great mistake of his reign was his entering into an alliance with, specifically King Ahab of Israel, in Ahab's unsuccessful attempt to recapture the city of Ramoth-Gilead (1 Kings 22:29-43; Crane, 1926. 1Kings 22:19-23). The relationship was further enhanced by having his son, Jehoram marrying Athaliah, daughter of Ahab and Jezebel (2 Kings 8:18, 27). Accordingly, Ahab's disputes now became family affairs for all of Israel. Jehoshaphat also helped Jehoram, King of Israel, in his battle with Moab (2 Chronicles 20:22-23). He made some religious reforms and reorganized the army. For two years before his father's death, he served as a co-regent with his father, Asa, when Asa became ill with a serious foot disease.

Jehoshaphat also introduced the system of local judges who decided and applied justice in fear of the Lord (Hindson, 2013, *text and annotation*, 19:5-11, pg.704). He likewise set up a system of appeals in Jerusalem where the chief Priest presided over spiritual matters. He also introduced a system whereby the King's civil officials administered civil matters (***ibids***).

His children included his son Jehoram, who became co-regent with his father Jehoshaphat (Hindson, 2013, *text and annotation*, 8:16, pg.606), as Eliezer the son of Dodavah of Mareshah prophesied, he had allied himself with the wicked Ahaziah the King of Israel to make ships go to Tarshish (2 Chronicles 36). For this, Eliezer told him, "Because thou hast joined thyself with Ahaziah, the Lord hath broken your works" (2 Chronicles 20:35-37), and by God's sovereign power, the ships were broken and did not go to Tarshish.

Jehoshaphat had many children, but it was Jehoram that succeeded him on the throne and is part of the Davidic Messianic line; others not so lucky included Azariah, Jehiel, Zechariah, Azariah, Michael, and Shephatiah (2 Chronicles 21:1-2). He reigned for about twenty-five years and died in about 847 B.C. (The Church of Jesus Christ of Latter-Day Saints, Wikipedia, 2020, pg. 538-539).

Jehoram/Joram

Jehoram was the son of Jehoshaphat and Athaliah, daughter of Ahab and Jezebel, the King of Israel (2 Chronicles 21:1). He was born c. 882 B.C. in Jerusalem. He was the fifth King of Judah (Jehoram of Judah – Wikipedia, 2020), taking the throne when he was thirty-two years old (2 Chronicles 21:5). He slew all his brothers and other princes

(2 Chronicles 21:4). Jehoshaphat "being then King of Judah, Jehoram the son of Jehoshaphat King of Judah ᵃⁱ"began to reign" (2 Kings 8:16). He thus became co-regent with his father around 852 B.C. to 848 B.C. and in his own right from 848 B.C. to 841B.C. (Hindson, 2013, *text and annotation,* 1:17, pg.593). He reigned for eight years in Jerusalem (2 Kings 8:17; 2 Chronicles 21:21).

He walked in the way of the King of Israel, like Ahab, doing evil in the eyes of the Lord. He built pagan worship places in Judah and led the residents to Jerusalem to commit sins (such as fornication) in the eyes of the Lord (2 Kings 8:18). So Elijah, a prophet, was sent by the Lord God to warn Jehoram about his evil deeds (2 Chronicles 21:12), as he was tolerating whoring, idol worship, and the massacre of his brethren, "which were better than" him (2 Chronicles 21:13). Elijah proclaimed (2 Chronicles 21:12), "Behold, with a great plague will the LORD smite thy people, and thy children, and thy wives, and all thy goods: And thou shalt have great sickness by disease of thy bowels until thy bowels fall out by reason of the sickness day by day" (2 Chronicles 21:14-15).

As if this were not enough, the Lord caused his enemies—including the Philistines, Arabians, and Ethiopians—to attack Judah and take away what he had in his house, including his wives and children, except for Jehoahaz/Ahaziah, the youngest (2 Chronicles 21:16-17). The final blow came when he was struck with an incurable disease in his bowel,[25] and "his bowels fell out by reason of his sickness: so, he diedᵃ of sore diseases. And his people made no ᵇburning for him, like the burning of his fathers... he reigned in Jerusalem eight years and departed without being desired..." (2 Chronicles 21:19-20).

His children included Ahaziah/Jehoahaz, his youngest son and the one chosen to continue in the Davidic Messianic line. All the older children—except for Jehosheba, Ahaziah's half-sister—were taken captive by the Philistines and others (2 Chronicles 21:16-17). Jehoram reigned from about 852–841 B.C. and died in c. 842/841 B.C. in Jerusalem at the young age of thirty-nine or forty years.

---

[25] Hindson, 2013, "a in great pain; b burning of spices; ai As coregent with his father.

Ahaziah/Jehoahaz

Ahaziah, or Jehoahaz, was the sixth King of Judah and the first Judahite to be descended from both the house of David and the house of Omri, King of Israel, through his mother, Athaliah, daughter of Ahab, King of Israel, and of Jezebel (2 Chronicles 22:2). He was Jehoram's youngest son to reign at the age of twenty- two (2 Kings 8:26) because he was the only one to escape being slain by the earlier Philistine and Arabian invasions (2 Chronicles 21:16, 17; 2 Chronicles 22:1).

His children included Jehoash/Joash or Joas. Even though the chronicler said he began his reign when he was forty-two (2 Chronicles 22:2), others note the proper age might really be twenty-two, "as read in the margin of the Hebrew Masoretic Text, 2 Kings 8:26, and several ancient versions of the Old Testament."[26]

Ahaziah ruled as his maternal grandfather, Ahab, did (2 Chronicles 22:3-4). He did evil in the sight of the Lord by remaining under the influence of his mother's paganism. He joined King Jehoram/Joram, son of Ahab of Israel, in fighting with Hazael, King of Syria, at Ramoth-Gilead (2 Chronicles 22:5) at the time that the Lord had appointed Jehu as King in Israel in place of Joram because of his evil ways (vv. 6-7). Jehoram fled when he saw Jehu, but he was pursued and slain. Ahaziah, who hid in Samaria, was also pursued and faced a similar fate as Jehoram when he was caught (vv.9). Eventually, he died at Megiddo, and his servants carried his body to Jerusalem, where he was buried (2 King 9:24-28).

Joash/Jehoash/Joas

Athalia, daughter of Ahab and Jezebel (2 Kings 8:18; Hindson, 2013, *Doctrinal footnote*, 22:10, pg. 709), usurped the throne after the death of Ahaziah: "When Athaliah the mother of Ahaziah saw that her son was dead, she arose and destroyed all the seed royal" (2 King 11:1). But Jehosheba/Jehoshabeath (2 Chronicles 22:11-12), Ahaziah's half-sister, took Joash, Ahaziah's son, and Zibiah of Beersheba said to have been born c. 843 B.C.(Ahaziah of Judah – Wikipedia, *en.m.wikipediaa.org*), and hid him along with his nurse. Joash was held in the "house of the

---

[26] Hindson, 2013, 22:2, pg. 708

Lord six years." (vv.12). Athaliah was eventually overthrown and killed (2 Chronicles 23: 12-15) by a revolt orchestrated by Jehoiada, the High Priest and Jehosheba's husband (2 Chronicles 22:11; 2 King 11:4-11; Hindson, 2013, *text and annotation*, 11:2, pg. 611). Only then was Ahaziah's rightful heir, and the one chosen to carry the Davidic line, installed King of Judah at the age of c.7/8 years.

Joash was the eighth King of Judah (Jehoash of Judah – Wikipedia,*en.m.wikipedia.org*) in the Davidic dynasty: Moreover, "Jehoiada, the priest . . . set all the people, every man having his weapon in his hand, from the right side of the temple to the left side of the temple, along by the altar and the temple... Then they brought out the King's son, and put upon him the crown, and gave him the testimony (the Law), and made him King. And Jehoiada and his sons anointed him, and said, God, save the King" (2 Chronicles 23:8-11).

According to the narrative in 2 Chronicles 24:1 and 2 Kings 12:1, he was seven years old when he began his reign, and he reigned for forty years. He did serve the Lord well by doing away with his grandmother's idol worship, rededicating holy objects in the Temple that had been used for the worship of Baal, and by repairing all the wickedness incurred by the high priest Jehoiada (2 Chronicles 24:5-14). Jehoiada even led the people in a covenant renewal and in spiritual rebirth and reformation.

Unfortunately, after the death of Jehoiada, Joash's mentor (2 Chronicles 24:17-18), Joash turned around by allowing the worship of idols back in Judah. Zechariah, High Priest and son of Jehoiada warned Joash of the wrath of the Lord. Joash didn't take this warning Kindly, so he had the people stoned the priest to death. Joash's "apostasy underscores the need for a personal faith that is characterized by a living fellowship with the Lord."[27]

Joash's servants, Jozachar, the son of Shimeath, and Jehozabad the son of Shomer, "conspired against him for the blood of the sons of Jehoiada, the priest, and slew him on his bed, and he died" (2 Chronicles 24:25; 2 Kings 12:21). He reigned from 835-796 B.C. (Hindson, 2013, *Ibid*, Pg. 538-539). The death occurred at Millo (Jehoash of Judah – Wikipedia, 2020), Jerusalem, in about 797/796 B.C., when he was forty-five or forty-six.

---

[27] Ibid, Hindson (2013), KJV, Text and annotation 24:17, pg. 711

Amaziah/Achaz/Ahaz

Amaziah ("**The strength of the Lord**"; or "**Yahweh is mighty**"), the ninth King of Judah (Amaziah of Judah - Wikipedia, 2020), was the son of Joash and Jehoaddan of Jerusalem. He was twenty-five years old when he began to reign (after the assassination of his father), and he reigned for twenty-nine years (2 King 14:1-4), of which twenty-four were as a co-regent with his son. He was considered a righteous King and was highly praised for executing his father's assassins while sparing their children as dictated by the law of Moses (2 Chronicles 25:3-4).

Amaziah launched an attack against the Edomites and defeated them after a man of God warned him; he should not use the hundred thousand mercenaries he hired from Israel: "O King, let not the army of Israel go with thee; for the Lord is not with Israel, to wit, with all the children of Ephraim. But if thou wilt go, do it; be strong for the battle: God shall make thee fall before the enemy: for God hath power to help" (2 Chronicles 25:5-8).

After Amaziah sent away the Israeli mercenaries, he went on and defeated the Edomites (2 Chronicles 25:10-12). However, those mercenaries came from behind him in anger and "fell upon the cities of Judah . . . and smote . . . them, and took much spoil" (2 Chronicles 25:11-13). Amaziah brought with him the idols of the Edomites and worshipped them (2 Chronicles 25:14). God sent him a Prophet to tell him he wasn't happy with what he did and would punish him for it (2 Chronicles 25:15). The punishment came sooner rather than later through King Joash of Israel, who defeated Amaziah's army at Beth-shemesh, entered Jerusalem, and plundered the house of the Lord, of gold, silver and all the vessels, including the treasures of the King's house and hostages (2 Chronicles 25:21-24). Amaziah escaped to Lachish due to a conspiracy against him in Jerusalem, but they followed him and slew him there (2 Chronicles 25:27).

His son with his wife, Jecoliah, Uzziah, inherited the throne after his death in 767 B.C. (2 Chronicles 26:1; Amaziah of Judah - Wikipedia, 2020; *Ibid, Hindson, 2013, K.J.V., Introduction to the first Book of Kings* pg. *538-539*). His entire reign ranged from 796–767 B.C., of which from 796-792 B.C. in regency with his son (*ibid*).

Uzziah/Azariah/Hizkiyahu

Uzziah/Azariah was the son of Amaziah and Jecoliah (Amaziah of Judah – Wikipedia, *en.m.wikipedia.org*). He was the tenth King of the ancient Kingdom of Judah, taking the throne at the age of sixteen after his father died (2 Chronicles 26:1). Of the fifty-two years he reigned, ten were in co-regency with his father, Amaziah, when he was imprisoned in the North—Israel (2 Chronicles 25:23-25), and another fifteen after his father's release (Hindson, 2013, *text and annotation*, 15:2, pg.617).

After co-regency, he had twenty-seven years of fully independent rule with great political success, peace, and prosperity (2 Chronicles 26:2, 6-15). In the beginning, Uzziah did what was acceptable in the eyes of the Lord and showed great interest in spiritual matters (2 Chronicles 26:3; 2 Chronicles 26:4,5), but pride and arrogance led him to think he could replace the High Priest in offering incense to the Lord in the Temple (2 Chronicles 26:16-19). Consequently, God cursed him with leprosy (v.19), and his son Jotham reigned with him as co-regent (Hindson, 2013, *text and annotation*, 15:5, pg. 617; 2 King 15:5; 2 Chronicles 26:19-21). While he was cursed, he lived alone, isolated from public activities (2 Chronicles 15:5). During this time, there was a real loss of spiritual vitality and genuine religion in Judah, as observed by some of the eighth century B.C. prophets of the southern Kingdom, such as Joel, Isaiah, and Micah. Uzziah reigned from about 783–742 B.C. or 791–739 B.C. When he died, he was buried in Jerusalem but excluded from the royal burial grounds.

Jotham/Yotam

Jotham was the son of King Uzziah with Jerushah/Jerusha, daughter of Zadok (2 Chronicles 27 :1; Jotham of Judah/Familypedia/Fandom; *familypedia.wikia.org; Wikipedia, en.m.wikipedia.org*), was the eleventh King of Judah. He reigned from 752 B.C. to 736 B.C. (Hindson, 2013 *Ibid*, pg.538-539), a period of sixteen years; eleven of which as co-regent (as a governor of the palace and the land) with his father for eleven years, ranging from 752/751 B.C. to 740/739 B.C. His reign began when he was twenty-five years old and reigned for sixteen years in Jerusalem (2 King 15:7, 32-38; 2 Chronicles 27). Jotham is said to have been a contemporary of the eighth-century prophets of the southern Kingdom including, Joel, Isaiah, Hosea, Amos, and Micah, who attest to the loss of spiritual vitality and genuine religion in Judah (Hindson, 2013, *Ibid* 15:5, pg.617; Micah 1:1; 2 Kings 15:34-35 and 2 Chronicles 27:2 say he did what was right in the sight of the Lord. He followed in his father's footsteps, even though the "High Places"—that is, pagan worship—continued unabated, and people still sacrificed burnt incense to idols. In general, it is said that he inherited a strong government, well officed, and administered. One of his achievements was the building of the upper gate of the Temple of Jerusalem. 2 Kings 15:37 mentions his wars against Rezin, the King of Syria, and Pekah, the son of Remaliah, King of Israel (vv.32), ruled from c. 740-732 B.C. (Hindson, 2013 15:25-27, pg.618).

Uzziah, his father, had defeated the Amorites and imposed an immense annual tribute. In the end, increasing corruption in the north Kingdom began to permeate Judah,[28] high places not removed, and Jotham was deposed by the pro-Assyrian faction in favor of his son Ahaz. Jotham is said to have died around 735 BC, and he was buried in Jerusalem.

Ahaz/Achaz

Ahaz was the twelfth King of Judah and the son of Jotham. He began his reign at the age of twenty as the twelfth King of Judah and reigned for sixteen years (Ahaz-Wikipedia, *Ibid*). He also served as a co-regent (Hindson, 2013, *text and annotation*, 5:37, pg. 619; Ahaz-Wikipedia, 2020) with his father, c.743 B.C. during the days of the conspiracy of Rezin, the King of Syria the Arameans and Pekah, the King of Israel (2 Kings 15:3)

According to 2 Chronicles 28:1-4, Ahaz did not do what was good in the sight of the Lord. He was a complete apostate. He walked in the ways of the King of Israel, corrupted and worshiping idols and offering sacrifices and burnt incense in the "high places" (2 Kings 16:4; Hindson, 2013 16:3,4). He even made molten images for Baalim (2 Chronicles 28:2) and "burnt his children in the fire, after the abominations of the heathen whom the LORD had cast out before the children of Israel. He also sacrificed and burnt incense in the high places, and on the hills, and under every green tree" (2 Chronicles 28 :3- 4). For these iniquities, he was delivered to the

---

[28] Hindson (2013), Places of pagan worship

Syrians as a captive: "they . . . carried away a great multitude of them captives, and brought them to Damascus. And he was also delivered into the hand of the King of Israel, who smote him with a great slaughter" (2 Chronicles 28:5).

Ahaz hired King Tilgath-pileser of Assyria, against the counsel of Prophet Isaiah, by paying him with silver and gold taken from the house of the Lord and in the treasures of the King's house (2 Kings 16:8). Tilgath-pileser responded and came to his aid and defeated both the Aramean/Syrians and Pekah, King of Israel, who was assassinated by pro-Assyrian forces in Israel. Ahaz presented himself as a vassal (Ahaz/ King of Judah; *britanica.com; Hindson, 2013, text and annotation 16:17, pg.620*) to the Assyrian King (2 Kings 16). The Lord was angered by Ahaz's bribe to Tilgath-pileser 111 when he was being pressured by Rezin and Pekah into an anti-Assyrian alliance. After the defeat of both Syria and Pekah, however, Ahaz was also attacked by the Edomites, who took some Judahites away as captives.

The Philistines also attacked, taking over some cities and occupying them, including Bethshemesh, Ajalon, Gederoth, Shocho, Timnah, and Gimzo (2 Chronicles 28:18). Tilgath-pileser harassed the King of Judah, causing him lots of distress and shame, and turning him into a vassal (2 Chronicles 28:19). "Ahaz took away a portion out of the house of the Lord, and out of the house of the King, and of the princes, and gave it unto the King of Assyria: but he helped him not" (2 Chronicles 28:21). To add insult to injury, he "sacrificed unto the gods of Damascus," which defeated him because he believed the gods of the King of Syria helped them: "Therefore will I sacrifice to them, that they may help me. But they were the ruin of him, and of all Israel" (2 Chronicles 28:23).

Ahaz practically became a vassal of the King of Assyria, who exacted a heavy annual tribute upon him (2 Chronicles 28:21). In short, Ahaz became an apologizing apostate (2 Kings 16:2-3) who not only allowed corrupting religious practices to flourish but participated in them himself (it was said he made his son walk through the fire of Moloch, one of the Phoenician idol gods. His son Hezekiah who inherited the crown after him, was said to have been saved from the flames of the idol by his mother: King Ahaz-Jewish...; *chabad.org*). Some of his heinous crimes involved sending children through the sacrificial fire as an offering to the Canaanite god, Baal. He destroyed all the vessels of the house of God by cutting them into pieces and "shut up the doors of the house of the Lord" (2 Chronicles 28:24). He introduced the worship of the Assyrian gods in the Temple in Jerusalem (*ibid*, vv.25).

When Ahaz died, he was buried in Jerusalem but not in the sepulchers of the Kings (*ibid*, vv.27). His sole reign lasted from 735–720 B.C. (Hindson, 2013, *Ibid*, pg.538-539), apart from his coregency in 743 B.C. with his father. His son Hezekiah became the godly link with the divine Davidic Messianic line after him.

Hezekiah/Hizqiyya

Hezekiah was the son of Ahaz with Abijah/Abi (2 Chronicles 29:2), the daughter of Zechariah, born about 739 B.C. (Hezekiah-Wikipedia, *en.m.wikipedia.org*) in Jerusalem. He reigned between 727–698 B.C. or 715–686 B.C. in Judah and was the thirteenth King of Judah (Hezekiah-Wikipedia, 2020) in the dynasty of David.

By all standards, he was considered a very righteous King (2 Kings 18:3); "...he did that which was right in the sight of the Lord, according to all that David his father had done" (2 Chronicles 29:2). He had co-regency with his father, Ahaz, in 729 B.C. (Hezekiah-Wikipedia, *en.m.wikipedia.org*) before beginning his sole reign from 716–697 B.C. He was also in co-regency with his son with Hephzibah, Manasseh, from c.697–687 B.C.

Hezekiah was completely loyal to the Lord of Israel (2 King 18:3-6). That such an apostate like Ahaz could have such a godly son was only by the grace of God. Ahaz led the degeneration into the worship of idols (2 Kings 16:10-18), but Hezekiah turned that around. He enacted sweeping religious reforms, including a strict mandate for the sole worship of Yahweh and a prohibition against venerating other deities within the Temple of Jerusalem (2 Chronicles 29:3-6; ch.30; 31:1; 31:2-19). He strengthened the defenses of his capital, Jerusalem (2 Chronicles 32:4,5; Crane, 1926. Hindson, 2013, *Doctrinal footnote*, 32:1, pg.722), and dug out the famous Siloam tunnel, which brought the water of the Gihon to a reservoir inside the city wall (Hindson, 2013, *text and annotation*, 20:20, pg.630; 2 King 20:20; 2 Chronicles 32:30). An inscription found near the Siloam tells of the excitement of the workers on the project, as they drew near to one another from opposite ends (Hindson, *ibid*).

Hezekiah witnessed the destruction of the Northern Kingdom of Israel by Sargon of Assyria in 722 B.C. Hezekiah also witnessed the siege of Jerusalem (Hindson, 2013, *text and annotation*, 19:29-31, pg. 628) by King Sennacherib of Assyria in 701 B.C. (he was not able to capture it). He was assassinated (2 Kings 19:37) in accordance with Isaiah's prophesy when he returned to his own country after mocking and blaspheming the Lord through Rab-shakeh, his chief aid.

Hezekiah was a contemporary of Isaiah, who prophesied the demise of King Sennacherib (assassinated by his own sons, Adrammelech and Sharezer, according to 2 Kings 19:37), as well as the coming Babylonian captivity, because Rab-shakeh had blasphemed the Lord by saying to the people let not Hezekiah deceive you... or make you trust in the Lord..." (2 Kings 18:29-30). On hearing this, Hezekiah sent Eliakim, the head of the household—Chief of Staff—to lead a delegation to Isaiah to find out what the Lord says, after hearing all the reproaches to the living God. Isaiah instructed them to tell Hezekiah; "Be not afraid of the words which thou hast heard. . . Behold, I will send a blast upon him . . . and I will cause him to fall by the sword in his own land" (2 King 19:1-7; Is. 39:6, 7; 2 Chronicles 32:22). Hezekiah was thus assured by Isaiah that God would deal with the blasphemous Sennacherib, and sure, when the blast came upon him, with a rumor of insurrection in his country, he returned only to be assassinated by his own children (2 Kings 19:37).

Hezekiah reigned from 729/8-699 B.C. (Hindson, 2013, **Outline of first kings**, Southern Kingdom, Pg.539) and died 699 B.C. at about the age of fifty-one or fifty-two, and was buried in Jerusalem "in the chiefest of the sepulchers"[29] (2 Chronicles 32:33) of the son of David, and all Judah mourned him.

Manasseh

Manasseh, the son of the righteous Hezekiah with Hephzibah, was born around c. 709 B.C. (Manasseh of Judah -Wikipedia, 2020). He was the oldest son 0f Hezekiah and began his reign as the fourteenth King

---

[29] Hindson (2013), Upper Tombs

of Judah at the age of twelve, reigning for fifty-five years, the longest of any of the old testament King (Hindson, 2013 21:1,2, pg.630) partly as co-regent with his father in 698/697 B.C. (2 King 21:1; 2 Chronicles 33:1; Hindson, 2013, *text and annotation* 20:19 Pg.630). His sole reign began around c.687/686 B.C. and continued until 643/642 B.C.

He was the first King of Judah who was not a contemporary of the Northern Kingdom of Israel, destroyed by the Assyrians in 722 B.C. (Manasseh of Judah - Wikipedia, 2020), where most of the people were deported. He didn't follow in the footsteps of his father, the righteous Hezekiah. Instead, he went back to the ways of his grandfather, Ahaz. He re-instituted polytheistic worship and reversed the religious changes made by Hezekiah. He vigorously reproduced the wickedness of Ahaz by bringing back the pagan altars into the various places of the Temple complex (2 Chronicles 33:1-6) and by placing the symbol of Asherah—the Canaanite goddess of fertility—within the Temple itself (Hindson, 2013, *text and annotation*, 21:1,2, pg.630).

God sent him numerous warnings to no avail (2 Chronicles 33:10). He shed much blood in Jerusalem, including that of the Prophet Isaiah. (According to Jewish and Christian tradition, (Hindson, 2013, *text and annotation,* 21:16, pg. 631; Hebrews 11:37), Manasseh might have sawed Isaiah into two.) The Lord God wasn't happy with Manasseh's evil at all: "And I will forsake the remnant of mine inheritance, and deliver them into the hand of their enemies, and they shall become a prey and a spoil to all their enemies (2 King 21:14).

According to 2 Chronicles 33:11-17, Manasseh might have been taken by the Assyrians into captivity and brought to Babylon by King Ashurbanipal in c.648-647 B.C., the year he occupied the throne, but he was later released and is said to have repented (2 Chronicles 33:11-17; Hindson, 2013, *text and annotation*, 21:17, pg.631). But whatever reforms he performed came too late, and they were too few to stop Judah's growing apostasy (Hindson, 2013, *Ibid*, pg. 631).

Manasseh had the longest reign in the history of Judah. In fact, his fifty-five-year reign was the longest of any of the Old Testament Kings (Hindson, 2013, *text and annotation*, 21:1,2, pg. 630). He died around c. 643/642 B.C. at the age of sixty-five or sixty-six and was buried "in the garden of his own house, in the garden of Uzza," not in the city of David among his ancestors (2 King 21:17-18; 2 Chronicles 33:20).

Amon

Amon was the son of Manasseh with Meshullemeth, the daughter of Haruz of Jotbah (2 Kings 21:19-20), born around c.664 B.C. in Jerusalem. He became the fifteenth King of Judah (Amon of Judah–Wikipedia, 2020), beginning his reign at the age of twenty-two and reigned from 642 B.C. to 640 B.C. (Hindson, 2013, **Southern Kingdom** pg. 539) a period of two years in Jerusalem. (2 King 21:19).

Amon is most remembered for his idolatrous tendency during his short two-year reign (Wikipedia, 2020, *ibid*). In fact, he was the most idolatrous ever; his religion was shown to be idolatry. His idolatrous practices led to a revolt against him and an eventual assassination in 640 BC: "And the servants of Amon conspired against him, and slew the King in his own house" (2 King 21:23; 2 Chronicles 33;21-24). This opened the door for his son (Josiah/Yoshiyahu) and Jedidah, his wife, daughter of Adaiah of Boscath, to take the throne when Josiah was only eight years old, and a period of spiritual concern arose in Judah (Hindson, 2013, *text and annotation*, 21:23, pg.631). When Amon died, he was buried in the garden of Uzza, as his father Manasseh had been.

Josiah/Yoshiyahu

Josiah began his reign at the tender age of eight and reigned for thirty-one years (2 King 22:1; 2 Chronicles 34:1). He was the sixteenth King of Judah (Josiah - Wikipedia, 2020), born around c. 648 B.C.in Jerusalem and reigning from around 640 B.C. to 609 B.C.

Unlike Amon, he instituted major religious reforms. At the age of twenty-six, he ordered that the Temple be repaired (2 Chronicles 34:8). He devoted his life to please God and instituted Israel's observance of the Mosaic Law, including the Passover (2 Chronicles 35:1-19; 2 King 23:1-25). He's credited by some Biblical scholars with having established or compiled important Hebrew Scriptures during the "Deuteronomic reform," which probably occurred during his rule (2 Chronicles 34:14-22).

King Josiah's record seems to appear only in Biblical sources or texts; no reference of him exists in other surviving texts of the period from Egypt to Babylon (Josiah -Wikipedia, 2020). Also, no explicit archaeological evidence of him exists (such as inscriptions bearing his name).

Josiah refused passage for Pharoah- Necho ll, King of Egypt, on his way to assist his Assyrian allies at Haran (Easton's Bible Dictionary *Biblestudytools*. The Assyrian capital, Nineveh, had fallen to an allied force that included the Chaldeans/Neo-Babylonians and Medes in c.612 B.C., forcing the Assyrians to move westward to Haran. Because of Egypt's long-standing allegiance to Assyria and a fear of a new Medo-Babylonian alliance, Pharoah Necho 11 was leading his army to Haran to link up with the Assyrians there. Josiah's attempt to prevent the Egyptians cost him his life (Crane, 1926. 2 Chronicles 35:20-25), but he did delay them long enough so that Haran fell before Pharoah- Necho 11 arrived (609 B.C.) (Hindson, 2013 23:28, 29. He joined the fight at the *valley of Megiddo* in disguise and was fatally wounded by a random arrow. His attendants carried him from Megiddo to Jerusalem (2 Kings 23:29-30; 2 Chronicles 35:24), where he was buried in his own sepulcher (vv.30) in c.609 B.C. The incidence is reported in 2 Chronicle 35:22-24 as follows:

> *"...came to fight in the valley of Megiddo. And the archers shot at King Josiah; and the King said to his servants, Have me away; for I am sore wounded. His servants . . . brought him to Jerusalem, and he died and was buried in one of the sepulchres of his fathers. And all Judah and Jerusalem mourned for Josiah.*

The Prophet Jeremiah and all the singing men and women lamented the death of Josiah (2 Chronicles 35:25).

Josiah had more children other than Jehoahaz/Shallum, his heir to the crown. These included Johanan (the elder), Eliakim/Jehoiakim (the second), Zedekiah/Mattaniah (the third), and Shallum (the fourth) with two wives, Zebudah, daughter of Pedaiah of Rumah, and Hamutal, daughter of Jeremiah of Libnah (2 King 23:31, 36; 1 Chronicles 3:15). Josiah died at the age of thirty-eight or thirty-nine, opening the way for his son Jehoahaz to begin his reign.

Shallum/Jehoahaz/Joahaz

Jehoahaz/Shallum ("Jehovah his sustainer" or "The Lord has grasped"), the son of Josiah with Hamutal, began his reign at the age of twenty-three (2 Kings 23:31) and was the seventeenth King of Judah (Jehoahaz of Judah, *Wikipedia, 2020*). He reigned for three months only in Jerusalem (2 Kings 23:31).

Although he wasn't the oldest of Josiah's children (two years younger than Eliakim; Easton's dictionary; *Biblestudytools*), he was the first to become King It is said he was as "brutal as a young lion" (*ibid*); his evil deeds were summed up in the following terms: "He did that which was evil in the sight of the Lord, according to all that his fathers had done" (2 King 23:32).

According to 2 Kings 23:31 and 2 Chronicles 36:1-2, he only reigned for three months in Jerusalem. He was deposed by Pharaoh- Necho 11 and carried to Egypt and imprisoned at Riblah (Hindson, 2013, *text and annotation*, 23:33-35, pg.635; Easton's dictionary *Biblestudytools.com/dictionary*). The pharaoh installed his brother Eliakim, son of Josiah with Zebudah, changed his name to Jehoiakim, and imposed a heavy tribute on him (2 Chronicles 36:3-4).

Jehoahaz never returned to Judah; he died a captive (2 Kings 23:34; Jeremiah 22; 10-12; Easton's Bible dictionary; *Biblestudytools*) just as it had been prophesied by Jeremiah. He was omitted from the genealogy of Jesus Christ.

Eliakim/Jehoiakim

Jehoiakim ("The Lord raises up" or "God raises up") was the second son of Josiah with Zebudah, the daughter of Pedaih of Rumah, and the second son of Josiah to become King of Judah (2 King 23:36). He was twenty-five years old when he began to reign and was the eighteenth King of Judah. (Jehoiakim-Wikipedia, 2020; *Wikipedia, 2020*).

Jehoiakim exacted silver and gold from the people to pay the tribute imposed upon him by Necho 11, the Pharaoh of Egypt (2 Kings 23:33-35; Crane, 1926. 2 Kings 24:1; Park 2014, pg.175). Unlike Josiah, his father, who did right in the sight of the lord for thirty-one years, practiced justice and righteousness and walked in all the way of his father David, "and turned not aside to the right hand or the left" (2 Kings 22:1-2; 2 Chronicles 34;1-2) and cherished the book of the law and before the word of God (2 Kings 22:11-14) and God blessed him with an abundance of food and clothing as well as success in all that he did(Jeremiah 22:15-16); his heart and desires were fixed on dishonest gains and greed. Prophet Jeremiah condemned his ambitions and vanity (Jeremiah 22: 13-16; 18-19). He was a tyrant who persecuted God's prophets. He killed Prophet Uriah, and Jeremiah barely escaped death at his hand. He cut the scroll of God's Word with a scribe's knife and burnt it.

In about 605 B.C., King Nebuchadnezzar of Babylon defeated Egypt, attacked Judah for the first time, and exercised his dominance over Jehoiakim (Hindson, 2013, *text and annotation*, 24:1, 24:2, pg.636). Three years later, Egypt and Babylon had another battle. This time, Egypt had the upper hand, and Nebuchadnezzar retreated to Babylon.

Jehoiakim had pledged his hope with Egypt in betrayal of Babylon. The Babylonians came back, and Egypt was not able to fend them off (2 Kings 24; 2-4). Nebuchadnezzar sent his army against Judah to destroy it (2 Kings 24:10-16); Hindson, 2013, *Ibid,* 24:10-16, pg.636; Dan. 1:2). Jehoiakim, according to 2 Chronicle 36:6) was bound in bronze chains and taken to Babylon (); Nebuchadnezzar took some of the articles in the house of the Lord to Babylon and put them in his temple (2 Chronicles 36:7).

Not long after being taken to Babylon, Jehoiakim returned to Judah and ruled for another eleven years (Park, 2014, page 179), until 597 BC. He did evil in the sight of the Lord and eventually died a miserable and tragic death at the young age of thirty-six, as prophesied by Jeremiah (Jeremiah 36:30; Jeremiah 22:18-19).

Gedaliah, the son of Ahikam (Hindson, 2013, *text and annotation*, 40:6, pg. 1124; Jeremiah 39:13-14) ------who saved Jeremiah's life from Jehoiakim----- was appointed governor by Nebuchadnezzar ll over those who remained in Judah after killing and taking many into captivity. Gedaliah also protected Jeremiah after the fall of Jerusalem (Jeremiah 40:5-6).

Jehoiakim is the second King to have had his name omitted from the genealogy of Jesus Christ.

Jeconiah/Coniah/Jechonias/Jehoiachin

Jehoiachin/Jeconiah ("Yah[30] has established; The Lord establishes") was the son of Jehoiakim with Nehushta, daughter of Elnathan of Jerusalem (2 King 24:8), a grandson of King Josiah. He became the nineteenth and penultimate King of Judah (Jeconiah-Wikipedia, 2020; *Wikipedia, 2020*) at the age of eighteen years. He was born between c. 615 B.C. or 605 B.C. (ibid); the date of his coronation is said to have been December 9 of 598 B.C. (*ibid),* when he was only eighteen years old (2 Kings 24:8).

Jehoiachin only reigned for three months and ten days; he did evil in the sight of the Lord and was dethroned by Nebuchadnezzar ll around March 15/16, 597 B.C. (2 Chronicles 36:9; Jeconiah-Wikipedia, 2020; *Wikipedia, 2020*). He was taken into captivity along with the cream leadership of Jerusalem, amongst whom were Ezekiel, the King's mother and wives, and the godly vessels of the house of the Lord (2 Kings 24:11-16; Ezek. 1:1; Hindson, 2013, *text and annotation*, 24:10-16, pg.636). This all happened, in part, because of King Jehoiakim's rebellion against Babylonian rule, which resulted in his dethronement and captivity in Babylon (2 Chronicles 36:5-8).

Records of Jeconiah's existence have been found on tablets in present-day Iraq (Jeconiah-Wikipedia, 2020; Wikipedia, 2020; see Hindson, 2013, *Ibid, 25:27-30*); they list his name among the recipients of food rations in Babylon. He reigned between December 9, 598 B.C., and March 15/16, 597 B.C. (Ibid, Hindson, 2013, *Ibid*, 25:27-30, pg.639).

Nebuchadnezzar ll died around 562 B.C. (*ibid, Hindson, 2013*) Shortly after, the new King, Nebuchadnezzar's son Evil-Merodach, released Jeconiah/Jehoiachin in his thirty-seventh year of captivity and granted him royal privileges, including "a continual allowance given him of the King, a daily rate for every day, all the days of his life" (2 King 25:30).

He died in Babylon and was succeeded by, "And the King of Babylon made Mattaniah his father's brother King in his stead, and changed his name to Zedekiah" (2 Kings 24:17); Zedekiah was Josiah's last remaining son (Hindson, 2013, text and annotation, 24:17-20, pg.637), that is his uncle. Apparently, the Davidic line from Jehoiachin/Jeconiah had been cursed by Jeremiah, saying that none of his offspring would sit "upon

---

[30] Hindson (2013), "Yah" is a shortened form of "Jehovah."

the throne of David" and "though Coniah the son of Jehoiakim King of Judah were the signet upon my right hand, yet would I pluck thee thence" (Jeremiah 22:24, 30). As such, none of his children or descendants inherited the throne; these included Assir, Salathiel/Sheatiel, Malchiram, Pedaiah, Shenazar, Jecamiah, Hoshama, and Nedabiah (1 Chronicles 3:17-18). He was recognized by the Jews in Exile as their last legitimate King

The Davidic covenant was confirmed on Salathiel/Shealtiel as the carrier of the Messianic line. It is said that Jehoiachin/Jeconiah was released from prison and placed above other King in exile on the thirtieth year of his captivity by, "that Evil-Merodach King of Babylon in the year that he began to reign did lift up the head of Jehoiachin King of Judah out of prison;...and set his throne above the throne of the King that were with him in Babylon; and changed his prison garments, and he did eat bread continually before him all the days of his life, and his allowance was a continual allowance given him of the King, a daily rate for every day, all the days of his life" (2 King 25:27-30; Jeremiah 52:31-34).

He was one of those who went to the Babylonians and surrendered in accordance with Jeremiah's prophesy that anyone who surrendered to Babylon would live. At the same time, those who resisted to the end would be captured and killed (Jeremiah 21:9, 27:8, 11-28). He is one of the persons mentioned in the genealogy Jesus Christ in (Matthew 1:11-12; see Table 1 in Appendix A).

Zedekiah/Mattaniah

Zedekiah ("The Lord is righteous") or Mattaniah ("The Lord's gift") was Josiah's son, and Hamutal, the daughter of Jeremiah of Libnah, and was his last remaining son. He was twenty-one years old when he began his reign in c. 597 B.C. (2 Chronicles 36:11; Zedekiah-Wikipedia, 2020; *Wikipedia, en.m.wikipedia.org*) after the deportation of Jehoiachin, his father's brother, and his nephew to Babylon. He reigned for eleven years in Jerusalem as the twentieth and last King of Judah (2 Kings 24:17).

He was a complete apostate and did evil in the sight of the Lord (Hindson, 2013 36:11, 12, pg.730) and was disrespectful of Jeremiah (2 Chronicles 36:12). He also rebelled against Babylon after taking an oath of allegiance by God: "He stiffened his neck, and hardened his heart from turning unto the LORD God of Israel" (2 Chronicles 36:13). Instead, he returned to the worship of idols (2 Kings 24:19).

Zedekiah's foolish rebellion was encouraged by the Egyptian Pharaoh Apries, who came to the throne of Egypt in c. 588 B.C. (Ezek. 17:15-17). Nebuchadnezzar besieged Jerusalem and built forts around it until there were famine and no bread. After Jerusalem fell (fulfilling Jeremiah 25:7-11), Nebuchadnezzar killed most of the Judahite princes and burnt most of the houses, taking the godly vessels in the house of the Lord and the King's house. He killed all of Zedekiah's sons right in front of him and plucked out his eyes before taking him, bound, to Babylon (2 King 25:3-7). Thus, began the Babylonian exile, and the dreadful prophesies of Jeremiah concerning Zedekiah were entirely fulfilled (Jeremiah 32:3-5, 34:1-3). Judah lost its status as a Kingdom and became a Babylonian vassal province (Jeremiah 40:5-6; Hindson, 2013, *text and annotation*, 40:6, pg. 1124; 2 Kings 24:4-12; 2 Chronicles 36:17-20).

The Lord God sent Zedekiah and the people messengers, but "they mocked the messengers of God, and despised his words, and misused his prophets, until the wrath of the Lord arose against his people, till there was no remedy" (2 Chronicles 36:16). Zedekiah rejected Prophet Jeremiah's advice to not fight against Babylon but to surrender. As a result of his insolence, he became the unfortunate King who saw the utter destruction of the Kingdom of Judah (2 King 25:1; Jeremiah 39:6-9). In short, he became a total apostate.

Unfortunately, he was the one who saw the final demise of a Kingdom that began around 930 B.C. and ended in 586 B.C., a period lasting 344 years. Zedekiah died in Babylon in c.561 B.C. (Zedekiah-Wikipedia, 2020; *Wikipedia, en.m.wikipedia.org*; Jeremiah 52:11).

Thus, among Josiah's four children, Shallum {Jehoahaz}, Eliakim {Jehoiakim, Jehoiachin's father} and Zedekiah {Mattaniah} who was the last to rule in Judah, only Johanan (Hindson, 2013, *text and annotation*, 36:11, 12, page 730), the firstborn, had not ruled in Judah (see Table 5 in Appendix E). The Southern Kingdom of Judah was deported to Babylon on three distinct occasions: the first in 605 B.C., the second in 597 B.C., and the third in 586 B.C. In accordance with God's promise, after 70 years in captivity, the Kingdom returned on three separate occasions as well. The first return was in 537 B.C., the second in 458 B.C., and the final one in 444 B.C.

CHAPTER IV

POST-EXILIC

Ancestors of Jesus Christ who were part of His genealogy
according to Matthew 1:1-16 who were never Kings of Judah

Salathiel/Shealtiel

Salathiel or Shealtiel ("I have asked of God") was one of Jechoniah's or
Jechonias' sons (1 Chronicles 3:17) who—as was most of the royal house
and elite of Judah—was exiled to Babylon by Nebuchadnezzar ll after
the siege of Jerusalem in 597 BC. Salathiel wasn't the physical son of
Jehoiachin/Jeconiah; he was only indirectly his child through Assir, his
son's daughter, who married Neri from the Davidic line of Nathan, "so
Salathiel was the son of Assir and Jeconiah/Jehoiachin, only through Assir's
daughter"[31] (2 King 24:6).

In Hebrew, the name means "I asked El" (for the child); this
acknowledges that the son is an answer to a prayer to God. There are
some conflicts in the Hebrew Scripture texts, however. For instance, in
1 Chronicles 3:19, Zerubbabel is listed as the son of Shealtiel's brother,
Pedaiah. In some other instances, Zerubbabel is listed as the son of
Shealtiel. There are some who think Zerubbabel could have been Shealtiel's
child legally but Pedaiah's biologically. This argument is based on the
Jews' levirate marriage or inheritance law (Deut. 25:5-6), which allowed
a brother to marry his brother's widow to provide a child for him. It's
possible that Shealtiel died (about 540 B.C., when he was between 37–54

---

[31] Hindson, 2013, text and annotation, 3:17, pg. 645

years old) childless, in which case Pedaiah would've married his widow and had Zerubbabel.

As an example, when Er, Judah's first son, died without a child, Judah asked his son Onan to marry Tamar so he could produce seed for his brother. But after marrying Tamar, Onan decided to "[spill] it on the ground" when he went in with her, saying he didn't want to give a seed to his brother. The Lord slew him for that act.

During the Babylonian captivity, Shealtiel was regarded as the Second Exilarch ("Head of the Diaspora" or "leader of the Jewish community in captivity" or "King-in-Exile"), following Jehoiachin, his father's death (2 King 25:27-30). Matthew 1:1 lists Salathiel/Shealtiel as the son who continued the Davidic line of Messianic prophesy. He was the second person in the third period of the genealogy of Jesus Christ (Matthew 1:12).

Zerubbabel/Zorobabel

In our discussion of Shealtiel or Salathiel, we pointed out that Zerubbabel (the meaning of name later) was born circa 566 B.C., was his son probably only through his brother, Pedaiah, who might have given him a seed according to the Jewish levirate or inheritance law. The purpose of such a law was to maintain the dead husband's name.[32] As such, Zerubbabel was a legal son of Shealtiel, as listed in Matthew 1:1-16 and Luke 3:23-38, and of Pedaiah by the flesh.

Zerubbabel and Jeshua/Joshua, son of Jozadak/Jehozadak, the high Priest, were among the leaders of the first band of Jew exiles, numbering 42, 360, from Babylon after captivity back to Jerusalem in the first year of Cyrus, King of Persia. Some scholars allege he might have been in King Cyrus's service under an Aramaic name, Sheshbazzar (Ezra 1:2).

While in captivity, he was the political leader of the tribe of Judah as a proud great-grandson and heir of King Jehoiachin. He was in direct line of the ancestry of Jesus (Matthew 1:12; Luke 3:27). His royal title in captivity was the third Exilarch in 545 B.C. This title was often considered that of "King-in-waiting," and it was first established following the deportation of

---

[32] Narrative citation Dr. Ayuba Mshelia (Wikipedia, 2020) (Personal communication), this was also practiced by some African tribes, including mine, the Bura of North East Nigeria.

Jeconiah/Jehoiachin (around 597 B.C.) into captivity by Nebuchadnezzar, King of Babylon. Consequently, his successor, Zedekiah, also held this title (around 587/586 B.C.).

After Babylon fell to Persia, Zerubbabel was appointed the eighth governor of Judah by Cyrus sometime between 537–536 BC (Haggai 1:1; 2:21). By proclamation, he allowed the Jews to go back to Judea and build the house (Temple) of the Lord. The Lord was pleased with Zerubbabel, so he sent Haggai, his prophet, to say, "I will take thee, O Zerubbabel my servant, the son of Shealtiel . . . and will make thee, as a signet: for I have chosen thee"(Haggai 2:23). As a governor of Judah, Zerubbabel was associated with the rebuilding of the second Temple and the prophets' ministry. Haggai promised him a special blessing, which had messianic implications (Haggai 2:21-23).

Zerubbabel's wives included a Babylonian princess, Amytis, who bore him Shazrezzar; Princess Rhoda of Persia, who bore him Rhesa/Reza; Esthra, a Jewish princess and Mavkab (Hitchcock Bible names dictionary, *Biblestudytools.com*, Easton's Bible Dictionary, *Biblestudytools.com*). His children and the basic meaning of their Hebrew names were listed as Meshullam ("friend, fellowship, reward") and Berechia ("The Lord blesses"), the fourth Exilarchs. Hananiah ("God has favored") was the fifth Exilarch. Then came Abihud/Abiud followed by Rhesa/Reza, Hasadiah/Hodaviah ("The Lord is King; goodness of the Lord"), Hashubah ("Consider; think deeply"), Ohel ("Tent"), Jushubhesed ("Love/grace will be restored"), and Shelomith ("Peaceful"), their sister (1 Chronicles 3:19-20).

Missing from the list of Zerubbabel's sons presented in 1 Chronicle 3:19-20) are Abiud/Abihud and Rhesa/Reza, even though both were listed in the genealogy of Jesus Christ by the two Gospels.

Abiud/Abihud

Abiud ("Father of glory," "Father of praise," or "Confession"; Hitchcock's Bible Names Dictionary, *Biblestudytools.com*; Easton's Bible Dictionary, *Biblestudytools.com*), a descendant of Zerubbabel, was referred to as Juda (Luke 3:26) and Obadiah (1 Chronicles 3:21). Abiud was the father of Eliakim (Matthew 1:13) and possibly the same as Obadiah (1

Chronicles 3:21). According to Matthew 1:13, Abiud/Abihud became the confirmed ancestor of Jesus in the Davidic line of the Messianic ancestry. He died around 510 B.C. (*ibid*), somewhere between 47–64 years old. He was the fourth person in the third period of Jesus Christ's genealogy (Matthew 1:12-13; see Table 1 in Appendix A).

Eliakim/Elyakim

Eliakim ("God establishes" or "God raises up"; "Father of glory," "Father of majesty") was the son of Abiud (Easton's Bible Dictionary, *Biblestudytools.com*). He was the fifth person in the third period of the genealogy of Jesus Christ (Matthew 1:13).

Azor

Azor ("Helpful; helper"; Hitchcock's Bible Names Dictionary, *Biblestudytools.com*), according to Matthew 1:13, was the son of Eliakim and a male descendant of the Messianic line. He was the sixth person in the third period of the genealogy of Jesus Christ (Matthew 1:13-14).

Sadok/Zadok

Sadok/Zadok ("Righteous, righteousness, justice"; Hitchcock's Bible Names Dictionary; *Biblestudytools.com*) was the son of Azor. Zadok lived c.280 B.C. (*ibid*) is mentioned in Matthew 1:14 as the male descendant in the Davidic Messianic line as the seventh person.

Achim/Jokim

Achim, a Hebrew short form for Jachin or Jehoiachin ("The Lord establishes"), was the son of Sadok (Smith's Bible Dictionary, *Biblestudytools. com*) and father of Eliud. He is the eighth person listed in the third period of Christ's genealogy by Matthew (1:14).

Eliud

Eliud ("God is my praise/glory; God of majesty") was the son of Achim and father of Eleazar (Smith's Bible Dictionary, *Biblestudytools.com*). He is the ninth person in the third period of Jesus Christ's genealogy (Matthew 1:14-15; see Table 1 in Appendix A).

Eleazar

Eleazar ("God has helped" or "Helped by God") was the son of Eliud (*ibid*). He is the tenth person in the third period of Jesus Christ's genealogy (Matthew 1:15).

Matthan

According to Matthew 1:15-16, Matthan ("Gift; offering") was the son of Eleazar (Easton's Bible Dictionary, *Biblestudytools.com*). He was also the father of Jacob, whose son Joseph became the earthly guardian, or foster-father, of Jesus Christ of Nazareth. In Luke 3:23-24, however, he is listed as the father of Heli, the father of Joseph. He was the eleventh person in the third period of the genealogy of Christ (Matthew 1:15).

Jacob/Yakob

Jacob is said in Matthew 1:16 to be the father of Joseph/Saint Joseph, the earthly foster-father of Jesus, the Messiah. His birthdate is estimated to have been between c. 53–25 B.C. and his death circa 20 B.C. He was the son of Matthan/Mattan with Hazibah/Estha, the grandson of Eleazar. Jacob was the husband of Gadat. His children are listed as Zachariah, Zadok, Saint Joseph, Ptolas, Alphaeus, Salome, and two others.[33] He is the twelfth person in the third period of Jesus Christ's genealogy (Matthew 1:15-16).

---

[33] Jacob - Wikipedia, 2020 (Wikipedia, 2020), Jacob ben Mattha, *geni.com*

Joseph/Saint Joseph

Saint Joseph was the earthly guardian or foster-father of Jesus and the spouse of Mary, the mother of Jesus, the Messiah. Joseph was the son of Jacob. In the Gospels, he's generally referred to as "from the house of David" (Matthew 1:15-16). He lived at Nazareth in Galilee (Luke 2:4). He was by trade a carpenter (Matthew 13:55). He was called a "just man" (Matthew 1:19). He is last mentioned in connection with the journey to Jerusalem when Jesus was twelve years old. He probably died before Jesus' public ministry. His name is not mentioned at the marriage feast in Cana of Galilee or all the events leading to the crucifixion (John 19:25).

Pope Pius IX proclaimed Saint Joseph, the Patron of the Universal Church in 1870. In other words, he is "the patron of a happy death." He is believed to have died "in the arms of Jesus and Mary." He's said to be the patron saint of many cities, including Austria, Belgium, Canada, Mexico, to name a few. It is believed the Spanish version, San José, is the commonplace name in the world. There are, to mention, a couple, San Jose, Costa Rica, and San Jose, California. He is the thirteenth person in the third period of Jesus Christ's genealogy (Matthew 1: 16).

Jesus Christ

Jesus Christ ("The Lord saves;" "He who will save His people from their sins," "help of Jehovah"; Smith's Bible Dictionary, *Biblestudytools. com*; "deliverer" Hitchcock's Bible Names dictionary {*ibid*}). The Messiah was conceived by the Holy Spirit and born through the body of the Virgin Mary (Matthew 1:18, 20, 23). Jesus the Christ is his official name to distinguish him from others so-called. He's also spoken of as "Jesus of Nazareth" (John 18:7), as well as "Jesus the son of Joseph" (John 6:42). He is the fourteenth and final person in the third period of his genealogy (Matthew1:16); (see also Table 1 in Appendix A).

CHAPTER V

THE GENEALOGY OF JESUS CHRIST ACCORDING TO LUKE 3:23-38

We will now begin our exploration of Jesus' genealogy, according to Luke. It is the same as Matthew's from Adam to Jesse, but he then follows Jesus' maternal genealogy through Nathan rather than Jesus' paternal genealogy through Solomon.

Nathan

Nathan (The name means "given" or "rewarded"; Hitchcock's Bible names Dictionary, *Biblestudytools.com*) was one of the youngest sons of King David and Bath-shua/Bathsheba (2 Samuel 5:14), the daughter of Ammiel (1 Chronicles 3:5). He was the third of four sons born to King David and Bathsheba in Jerusalem. His older brothers included Shimea/Shammuah, Shobab, and Solomon/Jedidiah ("Beloved of the Lord," born after the death of David's first child with Bathsheba, 2 Samuel 12:24).

He was the first child that Bathsheba was given the right to name, and she probably chose the name Nathan in honor of Prophet Nathan, her counselor. Her other children were named by King David and the Prophet Nathan.

Mattata/Mattathah

Mattata ("gift of Jehovah") was the only son of Nathan, born after 1014 B.C. (Smith's Bible Dictionary, *Biblestudytools.com*). He is listed in Luke 3:31 as one of the ancestors of Jesus through the line of Nathan (instead of the kingly Davidic line that went through King Solomon, Nathan's older brother).

Menan/Menna

Menan("numbered," "rewarded," or "prepared"; Hitchcock's Bible Names Dictionary, *Biblestudytools.com*) was the son of Mattata and father of Melea. In the Revised Version of the New Testament, he's called Menna.

Melea

Melea ("Fullness," "Supplying," or "Supplied") was the son of Menna and father of Eliakim; Easton's Bible Names, *Biblestudytools.com*) listed in the genealogy of Jesus (Luke 3:31).

Eliakim

Eliakim ("resurrection of God"; Hitchcock's Bible Names Dictionary, *Biblestudytools.com*)) was the son of Melea and father of Jonan/Jonam.

Jonan/Johanna/Jonam

Jonan ("Gift or grace of God," a dove" or "multiplying of the people"; Hitchcock's Bible Names Dictionary, *Biblestudytools.com*) was the son of Eliakim and a great-grandson of Nathan, born about c. 876 B.C.

Joseph

Joseph ("increase or addition"; Smith's Bible Dictionary, *Biblestudytools. com*) was the son of Jonan and listed in the genealogy of Christ (Luke 3:30)

Juda

Juda ("Praised"; Smith's Bible Dictionary, *Biblestudytools.com*; not Judah the son of Jacob/Israel) was the son of Joseph (Luke 3:30) and father of Simeon/Simen.

Simeon/Simen/Symeon

Simeon ("That hears or obeys" or "That is heard"; Hitchcock's Bible Names Dictionary, *Biblestudytools.com*) was the son of Juda (Luke 3:30).

Levi

Levi ("associated with him"; Hitchcock's Bible Names Dictionary, *Biblestudytools.com*) was the son of Simeon and the father of Matthat. The origin of the name is found in Leah's words in Genesis 29:34, which says, "This time will my husband be joined unto me."

Matthat/Matthan

Matthat/Matthan ("Gift of God") was the son of Levi and the father of Jorim. He was born circa after 623 B.C.; no exact date is known (Smith's Bible Dictionary, *Biblestudytools.com*).

Jorim

Jorim ("Whom Jehovah has exalted"; "he that exalts the Lord") was the son of Matthat and father of Eliezer (Hitchcock's Bible Names Dictionary, *ibid*).

Eliezer/ Eliezar

Eliezer ("God is help"; "help of God") was the son of Jorim and father of Jose (Easton's Bible Dictionary, *ibid*).

Jose/Joses/Joshua

Jose ("raised"; "who pardons") was the son of Eliezer and father of Er (Hitchcock's Bible Names Dictionary, *ibid*).

Er

Er ("Watchman") was the son of Jose and the father of Elmodam (*ibid*).

Elmodam/Elmadam

Elmodam ("The God of measure") was the son of Er and the father of Cosam (*ibid*).

Cosam

Cosam ("Diviner/divining") was the son of Elmodam and the father of Addi (*ibid*).

Addi

Addi ("Ornament") was the son of Cosam and the father of Melchi (*ibid*).

Melchi

Melchi ("My king" or "My counsel") was the son of Addi and the father of Neri (*ibid*; Easton's Bible Dictionary, *Biblestudytools.com*)

Neri/Neriah

Neri ("Jehovah is my lamp"; "Lamp of the Lord") was the son of Melchi and the father of Salathiel (Hitchcock's Bible Names Dictionary, *ibid*).

Salathiel/Shealtiel

Salathiel ("I've asked of God" or "Lent of God"; Smith's Bible Dictionary, *Biblestudytools.com*) was both the son of Neri and also, legally, the son of Assir (1 Chronicles 3:17; Hindson, 2013, *text annotation*, 3:17-3:19, pg. 645) and Jeconiah/Jehoiachin through Assir's daughter who married Neri of the line of Nathan, the son of David. Hence, both Gospels—Matthew 1:12 and Luke 3:27—mention him as an ancestor of Jesus Christ. Matthew mentions him as a descendant through Solomon and Luke as a descendant through Nathan.

In both Gospels, Zerubbabel is listed as Sheltiel's son, even though 1 Chronicles 3: 19 mentions him as the son of Pedaiah, Sheltiel's brother. The genealogical lists in both Gospels found a common meeting ground in both Sheltiel and Zerubbabel. Sheatiel grew up in a foreign land (Babylon), having to endure all sorts of pain and sorrow, ultimately died without a child, hence by levirate law (Deut.25:5-10; Matthew 22:23-33 and Luke 20:28) Pedaih his brother took his sister-in-law and bore him a son, Zerubbabel (Hindson, 2013, *Ibid, 3:19, page 645*). The purpose of such levirate marriage was to maintain the dead husband's line; hence Zerubbabel is legally the son of Salathiel

Zerubbabel/Zorobabel

Zerubbabel ("Born at Babel"—Smith's Bible Names; "Born in Babylon"—Park 2014; "descendant of Babylon"—ibid; "the seed of Babylon"—Easton's Bible Dictionary; "stranger at Babylon"---Hitchcock's Bible Names) as explained before, was born around 566 B.C.(Zerubbabel., 3rd Exilarch; *Geni.com*) and was only a legal son of Salathiel and, therefore, the grandson of Jehoiachin (the penultimate King of Judah who was taken captive by Nebuchadnezzar in about 598 B.C., 1 Chronicles 3:17) but, biologically, the son of Pedaiah through the levirate law. Zerubbabel—along with Jeshua/Joshua, son of Jozadak/Jehozadak, the high priest—was a leader of the exiles, called the third **Exilarch** (a natural heir to Jehoiachin), who later returned from the Babylonian captivity to Jerusalem along with many others in the first wave, numbering about 42,360 exiles

(Ezra 2:2; Nehemiah 12:1), in the first year of King Cyrus of the Persian Empire.

Zerubbabel's royal title in captivity was that of the third Exilarch.[34]

Some scholars have alleged he might have been in King Cyrus's service under an Aramaic name, Sheshbazzar (Ezra 1:1-8).

Zerubbabel was appointed a governor of Judah by King Cyrus (Haggai 1:1), and he was involved in the building of the second Temple (with Joshua) and in the restoration of worship to the Lord of Israel. Zerubbabel was also involved with the ministry of the prophets Haggai and Zachariah (Ezra 5:1, 2).

The Lord of Hosts was pleased with Zerubbabel's efforts in bringing Israel back to their God. This is supported by the following: "On that day, says the Lord of hosts, I will take you Zerubbabel, son of Sheltiel, my servant, and wear you like a signet ring; for it is you whom I have chosen. This is the word of the Lord of hosts" (Haggai 2:23).

His wives were Amytis, a Babylonian princess who bore him Shazrezzar; Princess Rhoda of Persia, who bore him Rhesa/Reza; Esthra, a Jewish princess and Mavkab. His children were Reza/Rhesa, Meshallum, Hananiah, Abiud, Berechiah, Hashubah, Ohel, Hasadiah, Jushab-hesed, Sheconiah, Rephasiah, Arman, Obadiah, and their sister, Shelomith (1 Chronicles 3:19-20). He died in about 510 B.C., when he was between 47–64 years old. In Luke 3:23-38, his son Rhesa/Reza is listed in the Davidic messianic line through Nathan (see Table 2 in Appendix B).

Reza/Rhesa

Rhesa ("Affection"; Easton's Bible Dictionary, *Biblestudytools. com; "head"*; Smith's Bible Dictionary, *ibid*) is one of the many sons of Zerubbabel that is listed in Luke 3:27 as the ancestor of our Lord Jesus Christ from the line of Nathan.[35]

---

[34] Narrative citation Dr. Ayuba Mshelia (Wikipedia, 2020) To recap, the first Exilarch was Jehoiachin and the second Shealtiel.

[35] Narrative citation Dr. Ayuba Mshelia (Wikipedia, 2020) A different son, Abiud/Abihud, was mentioned in Matthew 1:1-16 as the ancestor of Jesus Christ in the Davidic line of the Messiah through the line of Solomon

Joanna/Johanan

Joanna ("Whom Jehovah has graciously given" or "bestows"; "grace" or "gift"; Easton's Bible Dictionary, Hitchcock's Bible Names Dictionary, *ibid)* was the son of Rhesa and grandson of Zerubbabel, as well as the father of Joda/Juda. Some scholars have suggested this is the same as Hananiah, mentioned in 1 Chronicles 3:19 as the son of Zerubbabel.

Juda/Joda

Juda was the son of Joanna, and the father of Joseph mentioned in Christs' maternal ancestry. Some scholars have alleged this might be the same as Abiud (Matthew 1:13) or even Obadiah (1 Chronicles 3:21; Easton's Bible Dictionary, *Biblestudytools.com*).

Joseph/Josech

Josech/Joseph (Revised version for Joseph, in NET, AVS, NRSV, NASB) was the son of Juda (*ibid*) and father of Semei/Semein. He is said to have been born between 536 and 410 B.C. Other two people with the same name were mentioned in the ancestry of Jesus Christ (Luke 3:24, 30).

Semei/Semein

Semei (Semein in the Revised version; "Hearing" or "obeying," and the Greek form is Shimei, Esth. 11:2; Easton's Bible Dictionary and Hitchcock's Bible Names Dictionary, *Biblestudytools.com*) was the son of Joseph and the father of Mattathias.

Mattathias/Mattathiah

Mattathias ("Gift of Jehovah") was the son of Semei (Luke 3:26) (Easton's Bible Dictionary, *Biblestudytools.com*) and the father of Maath. Lived after circa 406 B.C. (Smith's Bible Dictionary, *ibid*).

Maath

Maath ("Small"; "wiping away," "breaking," "fearing," "Smiting"; Easton's Bible Dictionary and Hitchcock's Bible Names Dictionary, *Biblestudytools.com*) was the son of Mattathias and the grandson of Semei.

Nagge/Naggai

Nagga-i/Nagge (Nagge in the Revised version; "Illuminating," "clearness," "brightness," "light"; Smith's Bible Dictionary; Easton's Bible Dictionary and Hitchcock's Bible names Dictionary, *Biblestudytools.com*) was the son of Maath and the father of Esli and grandson of Mattathias.

Esli

Esli ("Near me" or "He who separates"; Hitchcock's Bible Names Dictionary, *Biblestudytools.com*) was the son of Nagge and the father of Naum/Nahum (Luke 3:25). Esli ben Nagge was born circa 273 B.C. (Esli ben Nagge - familypedia, Wikipedia, 2020).

Naum/Nahum

Naum/Nahum ("Consolation; comforter; penitent"; Hitchcock's Bible Names Dictionary, *Biblestudytools.com*) was the son of Esli and father of Amos (Luke 3:25). He was a contemporary of the high priesthood of Jason during the reign of Antiochus Epiphanes in about 175 B.C. (Smith's Bible Dictionary, *Biblestudytools.com*)

Amos

Amos ("Loading; weighty" or "Burden"; *ibid)* was the son of Naum and the father of Mattathias (Luke 3:25).

Mattathias/Mattathiah

Mattathias ("the gift of the Lord"), born after 406 B.C.(Smith's Bible Dictionary, *Biblestudytools.com*) He was the son of Amos mentioned in (Luke 3:25; Easton's Bible Dictionary, *ibid*).

Joseph

Joseph ("Increase; addition") was the son of Mattathias in the genealogy of Jesus Christ in Luke's gospel (Luke 3: 24) and born after circa 400 B.C. (Smith's Bible Dictionary, *Biblestudytools.com*).

Janna/Jonan/Jannai

Janna ("Flourishing") was the son of Joseph and the father of Melchi (Luke 3:24; Hitchcock's Bible Names Dictionary, and Smith's Bible Dictionary, *Biblestudytools.com*). Jannai is the name used in the Revised Version.

Melchi

Melchi ("My King; my counsel") was the son of Janna and the father of Levi (Luke 3:24; Hitchcock's Bible Names Dictionary, *ibid*).

Levi

Levi ("Associated with him"; *ibid*) was the son of Melchi and the father of Matthat (Luke 3:24).

Matthat

Matthat ("Gift of God") was the son of Levi. One of the early Church historians, Sextus Julius Africanus, in his third-century *Epistle to Aristides*, when explaining the origin of Joseph from levirate law, refers to him as Melchi, a papponymic naming after his grandfather, which was a very common practice then and is sometimes practiced even today. Another Church historian, St. J. Damascene, in *An Exact Exposition of the Faith*,

Book 4, Chapter IV, wrote, "Concerning our Lord's genealogy and concerning the holy Mother of God," which seemed to imply the same: "Levi begat Melchi . . ." (see Table 4 in Appendix D).

Heli/Eli

Heli/Eli ("Elevation"; "ascending/ascension"; "climbing up") was the son of Matthat/Melchi and the father of Joseph the husband of the Virgin Mary (Luke 3:23), and perhaps the grandfather of Mary herself (Smith's Bible Dictionary, *Biblestudytools.com*).

Joseph

A reputed Foster- father of our Lord (Luke 3:23), he lived at Nazareth in Galilee (Luke 2:4). He is called a "just man and by trade a carpenter or stonemason (Matthew 13:55). He is last mentioned in connection with the journey to Jerusalem when Jesus was twelve years old; and was apparently absent at the marriage feast in Cana of Galilee, given that only Mary was mentioned. His name does not appear in connection with the scenes of the crucifixion along with that of Mary (John 19:25; Easton's Bible Dictionary, *Biblestudytools.com*).

In Luke 3:23, it is written, "And Jesus himself began to be about thirty years of age; being (as was supposed) the son of Joseph, which was the ***son*** of Heli" (emphasis added). The use of the words "as was supposed" by Luke has created a lot of controversy since the days of the early traditional Church leaders, such as Africanus and Eusebius, because it creates an impression that the Gospel message is not infallible. However, it could be argued that Luke used the phrase also because of Christ's Virgin birth. The use of the phrase "as was supposed" and the differences in the two lists led to the question of the accuracy of the gospel accounts especially, the criticisms coming from the Manichaeans (an elaborate third century A.D. dualistic cosmology teaching describing the struggle between a good, spiritual world of light, and an evil, material world of darkness). Augustine, for instance, attempted on several occasions to refute every criticism, especially coming from the Manicheans.

Jesus

Jesus ("Yahweh is salvation", Hindson 2013, *text and annotation*, 1:31, page 1485; "Savior," "help of Jehovah," Smith's Bible Dictionary; "deliverer," Hitchcock's Bible Names Dictionary, *Biblestudytools.com*). Jesus the Christ is the official name of our Lord to distinguish him from others so-called, he's spoken of as "Jesus of Nazareth" (John 18::7) and "Jesus the son of Joseph" (John 6:42; Easton's Bible Dictionary, *ibid*). The name Jesus used for himself was "Son of Man" (John 11:30,12:34; Luke 12:8, 10, 40). The name emphasizes his Messianic office and uniquely identifies his humanity (Hindson 2013, *Doctrinal footnote* 1:51, page 1552, cf. Acts 7:56). As Messiah he fulfills three anointed offices of Prophet (Myrrh—a valuable ointment), Pries (Frankincense--- a valuable perfume) and King (Gold---- valuable currency). For the believers sanctified in Christ, his being a Prophet means he's our spokesman for God; as a Priest he's our representative before God and as a King he's the ruler in the lives of God's elect (ibid).

CHAPTER VI

A SYNTHESIS AND SUCCINCT PURVIEW OF THE GENEALOGIES IN THE TWO GOSPELS

The Bible, as God's inspired Word and a reference book, is, in part, filled with the history of holy genealogies which anticipate the "seed of the woman." It began with Adam and Eve and continued through the godly lineage of the **called**, both in the Kingly/royal and ordinary lines of David (Mal. 2:15; see also Tables 1 and 2).

However, before we go any further, let's define what genealogy is. Genealogy is "a record that charts out patrilineal descent of a clan that originates from a single ancestor.[36] This means it is the family's historical account that reveals the clan's origin while honoring its blood descent and lineal succession.

The Bible unambiguously testifies to the importance of genealogy to the Jewish culture and people for thousands of years as a summary of their ancestral history and God's history of redemption (Genesis 47:9; Deut. 26:7; 1 Chronicles 29:10). This is especially true of the priestly class, where Josephus, the ancient Jewish historian, observed that for the priesthood, the genealogy was strictly and meticulously managed for over a period of two thousand years.

Jesus Christ's genealogy, as presented in both the Gospel of Matthew (1:1-16) and Luke (3:23-30), is a great testimony to how meticulously

---

[36] Park, 2014, pg. 65

genealogies are perceived by the Jews. This is true even after their return from the Babylonian captivity, where "Ezra and Nehemiah thoroughly reviewed, supplemented, and organized their genealogies."[37]

Genesis Genealogies

The Bible contains various forms of genealogies. For instance, the book of Genesis contains ten genealogies, which present God's extensive history of redemption and salvation. As a matter of fact, the book of Genesis is nicknamed the "book of genealogies." The ten genealogies seem to be separate from one another, but, in essence, they're all connected. When one ends, the next one starts immediately. According to Park, these are the summaries of the genealogies in Genesis, which seem to separate but actually form a whole:

1.   The genealogy of the heavens and the earth (1:1–2:4; 2:4–4:26)
Genesis 1:1 *This is the account of the heavens and the earth when they were created.*

2.   The genealogy of Adam's generations (5:1–6:8)
Genesis 5:1 *This is the book of the generation [Hebrew representation symbol] of Adam.*

3.   The genealogy of Noah's family (6:9–9:29)
Genesis 6:9 *These are the records of the generations [Hebrew representation symbol] of Noah.*

4.   The genealogy of Noah's sons (10:1–11:9)
Genesis 10:1 *These are the records of the generations [Hebrew representation symbol] of Shem, Ham, and Japheth, Noah's sons.*

5.   The genealogy of Shem (11:10-26)
Genesis 11:10 *These are the records of the generations [Hebrew representation symbol] of Shem.*

---

[37]   Ibid, pg. 67; Ezra 9-10; Neh 13

6.   The genealogy of Terah Abraham (11:27–25:11)

Genesis 11:27 *These are the records of the generations [Hebrew representation symbol] of Terah.*

7.   The genealogy of Ismael (25:12-18)

Genesis 25:12 *These are the records of the generations [Hebrew representation symbol] of Ismael, Abraham's son.*

8.   The genealogy of Isaac (25:19–35:29)

Genesis 25:19 *These are the records of the generations [Hebrew* representation symbol] *of Isaac, Abraham's son.*

9.   The genealogy of Esau (36:1–37:1).

Genesis 36:1 *These are the records of the generations [Hebrew representation symbol] of Esau (that is, Edom).*

10-The genealogy of Jacob (37:2–50:26)

Genesis 37:2 *These are the records of the generations [Hebrew representation symbol] of Jacob.*

Genealogies in Chronicles

First Chronicles begins with genealogies and continues through chapter 9. The genealogies in Chronicles cover a period of over 3,600 years, starting from Adam until the second return from the Babylonian captivity. The genealogy covers Adam, Noah, Abraham, Jacob, David, and others involved in the ratification of essential covenants (1 Chronicles 1:1-4, 5, 8, 17, 24-27; 2:1; 3:1).

The book of Chronicles, which opens with genealogy, comes toward the end of the Hebrew Bible. The gospel of Matthew, which also starts with the genealogy of Jesus Christ, comes at the beginning of the New Testament. This signifies that genealogies connect the book of Chronicles in the Old Testament with the Gospel of Matthew in the New Testament.

The genealogy in 1 Chronicle shows God's work of redemption/ salvation within the history of the Jewish people, while those of Matthew and Luke are about Jesus Christ, revealing how God's redemptive work of history is fulfilled without failure through his son, Jesus Christ.

A cursory review of the entire genealogies in Chronicles shows a distillation of the Jewish people's history starting from Adam. If the Genesis genealogies are centered on Abraham and on Jacob's twelve sons, then one of the Chronicles is centered on David and the remnant returning to Jerusalem from Babylon, led by Zerubbabel and Joshua and, later, Ezra and Nehemiah.

The extensive genealogies in the book of Chronicles act as a bridge that connects the past to the future of the Jewish people returning from captivity after seventy-year bondage in Babylon.

On the other hand, the genealogy in the book of Ruth (4:18-22) is important because it points to the Messiah as coming from the descendant of David. The list of the ten generations in Ruth above—from Pharez, Judah's illegitimate son with Tamar, a Canaanite, to David—seems to reflect the constraints or prohibitions (regarding persons excluded from the congregation due to improper sexual conduct, such as bastards/illegitimate children or any violation of the sacrosanct nature of the family through adultery) in Deuteronomy 23:2. It serves to legitimize David's claim to the throne of Israel through the union of Boaz, a Judahite, and Ruth, a gentile woman.

It was God's divine plan that Jesus Christ would come through the descendants of a gentile woman and a Jew, one from among his chosen people. This union thus anticipates the church through whom all believers become one. This genealogy serves as a link between the dark period of the Judges and the King Despite the spiritual decadence during the Judges' period, the genealogy in Ruth 4 gives hope that God has continued to prepare the Davidic lineage and the Messiah who will come, unfailingly, as his descendant.

CHAPTER VII

GENEALOGY OF CHRIST ACCORDING TO MATTHEW 1:1-16

The two genealogies of Matthew and Luke in the New Testament are harmonized, as already presented above. The two accounts have been streamlined from Adam to David, and they vary only from David to Joseph (see Table 1 in Appendix A). The reason for such a streamline has already been discussed previously, so it will not be repeated here.

While the Matthean genealogy (see Table 1 in Appendix A) in his Gospel lists forty-one persons from Abraham to Jesus in a linear order, the genealogy in Luke lists seventy-seven persons from Jesus to Adam in ascending order. The genealogy in Luke 3 provides a sweeping view of the story of redemption that links Jesus Christ, the Spiritual man, to Adam, the Earthman.

What I intend to do is try and harmonize both Matthew and Luke in terms of their human generation direction (Adam to Jesus) and in terms of Spiritual perspective (from Adam the Earthman to Jesus the Spiritual man). Jesus Christ had no beginning and no end. Hence, it's proper to view him as continuing forever; he's self-existing from everlasting to everlasting (Heb. 1:12; 7:24; 13:8).

Matthew has twenty-seven generations from David to Joseph, and Luke has forty-two with almost no overlap. The disagreement between the two genealogies about Joseph's father has been a thorn since ancient times, and it is now explored through levirate marriage (see Tables 3 and 5).

Ever since Saint Jerome translated the Hebrew Bible in about 340/405

A.D. into the **Vulgate**, traditional Christian scholars—starting with Sexton Julius Africanus, Eusebius, and Damascene—have put forward some postulates that seek to explain the differences, but they've found little success. There was no consensus about whether or not the lineages are both of Joseph or of Mary and Joseph or both of Mary. Most seemed to ascribe Luke's to Mary and Matthew's to Joseph. There are some modern scholars who seem to suggest both genealogies are "bogus" and an invention, purposely created to bring the Messianic covenant into conformity with the Jewish Biblical Messianic claims and prophecies.[38]

Matthew's Gospel has fourteen generations from Abraham to David and fourteen generations from David to the deportation to Babylon. He also has fourteen generations from the deportation to Babylon until the coming of Jesus Christ in 4 B.C., giving us a total of forty-two generations (Matthew 1:17). Matthew presented Jesus from the beginning as the anointed one—that is, as a King, the Messiah, and a descendant of King David. He started out by calling him "son of David," thus emphasizing his royal lineage, and "son of Abraham," again indicating he was an Israelite (both are used as stock phrases). Although Jesus' paternal ancestors through Joseph include Jehoiachin, the line of descent is recorded only to show Jesus' legal right to the **throne of David** (Matthew 1:11-16).

This was "because Jesus was Virgin-born, hence not the natural son of Joseph, the pronouncement against Jehoiachin's line is not, contradicted"[39] (cf. Matthew 1:18; Luke 1:34-38). As I mentioned before, it is also worth noting that Jesus' human descent is traced through Mary—a descendant of David through his son Nathan—and not through Solomon (Luke 3:23-31; see Table 4 in Appendix D). Thus, he is heir to the throne from both parents.

The Matthean genealogy from Abraham can be seen as being divided into three categories. The first category seems to be rich in annotations, including four mothers—Tamar, Rahab/Rachab, Ruth, and Bathsheba— and mentioning the brothers of Judah and Selah/Zerah, the brother of Pharez/Perez (1 Chr. 2:4). The second category seems to span the Davidic royal line, but it omits several generations (see the section on Omissions and Tables 5 and 6), including Jeconiah/Jehoiachin and his brothers at

---

[38] Borg and Crossan, 2009, pg. 95

[39] Hindson, 2013, *text and annotation*, 22:30, pg. 1095

the time of the deportation/exile. The third and final category of fourteen generations connects Zerubbabel to Joseph and many other unknown names.

Some have posited the question of why the Matthean genealogy, which went through King Solomon, has about exactly forty-two generations, inferring that it's deliberately done to achieve a gematria favorable to David or because fourteen is twice seven, which they deem as symbolizing perfection and covenant.

However, if Matthew had intended anything but a truthful list, he would have made it anything but forty-two. The number of forty-two could also be conceived in different ways. For example, it could be interpreted as representing twice of triple sevens (777, 777), symbolizing the threefold perfection of the trinity, as contrasted against triple 666, the number of the Beast (Hindson, 2013, *text and annotation*, 13:16-18, page 1919).

Thus, to read anything ulterior to Matthew's forty-two generations is to seek to create a dispute where dispute doesn't exist. Matthew could have included the omitted Kings (see Table 5 in Appendix E) despite their evil records because none of those included were perfect human beings and, as the Lord God told Moses, "I will be gracious to whom I will be gracious, and I will shew mercy on whom I will shew mercy" (Ex. 34:19).

But the choice was not Matthew's to make; it was God's, who had "foreknown and called" whom he had planned from the beginning to be included in the genealogy of his son. The Bible is the inspired Word of God through the redemption work of the Spirit of Truth. Jesus said, "Comforter which is the Holy Ghost, whom the Father will send in my name, he shall teach you all things and bring all things to your remembrance whatsoever I have said unto you" (John 14: 26).

Patrilineage of Jesus Christ according to Matthew 1:1-16

GOD				
1. Adam	15. Heber	29. Naasson/ Nahshon	43. Ahaz	57. Eleazar
2. Seth	16. Phalec	30. Salmon and Rahab/ Rachab	44. Hezekiah	58. Matthan
3. Enos	17. Ragau	31. Boaz and Ruth	45. Manasseh	59. Jacob
4. Cainan	18. Saruch	32. Obed	46. Amon	60. Joseph
5. Maleleel	19. Nachor	33. Jesse	47. Josiah	61. Jesus
6. Jared	20. Thara/ Terah	34. David and Bathsheba	48. Jeconiah/ Jehoaichin	
7. Enoch	21. Abraham	35. Solomon	49. Shealtiel	
8. Mathusala	22. Isaac	36. Rehoboam	50. Zerubbabel	
9. Lamech	23. Jacob	37. Abijah	51. Abihud	
10. Noah	24. Judah and Tamar	38. Asa	52. Eliakim	
11. Shem	25. Phares/ Perez	39. Jehoshaphat	53. Azor	
12. Arphaxad	26. Esrom/ Hezron	40. Jehoram	54. Zadok	
13. Cainan	27. Aram/Ram	41. Uzziah/ Azariah	55. Achim	
14. Shelah	28. Amminadab	42. Jotham	56. Eliud	

CHAPTER VIII

GENEALOGY OF CHRIST ACCORDING TO LUKE 3:23-38

In the beginning, I indicated I would adopt Luke's format (see Table 2 in Appendix B) of including Adam but going in the opposite direction. Instead of ascending from Jesus to Adam, I reversed the direction to descend from Adam to Jesus. This means both genealogies flow from Adam to Abraham. Still, they differ significantly in terms of the generations listed from David to the first deportation to Babylon and the post-exilic period to Jesus.

One of the controversies with Luke's Gospel presentation since the ancient time is the following: After telling of the baptism of Jesus, Luke 3:23-38 states, "Jesus himself began to be about thirty years of age, which was [the son] of Heli," and it continues on until "Adam which was [the son] of God" (3:23, 38). Some have argued that in the original Greek text of Luke's Gospel, he does not use the word "son" in the genealogy after "son of Joseph."[40] Robertson notes that, in the Greek version, "Luke has the article *tou* repeating *Uiou* (son) except before Joseph."[41]

Luke's genealogy descends from the Davidic royal line through Nathan, who is relatively unknown. It is expedient for Luke not to actually say "son of Joseph" because of the Virgin birth. Joseph is an adoptive father, a position arguable in Jewish Law.

---

[40] Robertson, Wikipedia, 2020 "Commentary on Luke 3:23
[41] Ibid

Augustine notes that the generation count in Luke is seventy-seven, a number representing the forgiveness of all sins.[42] [43] [44] This count agrees with the seventy generations from Enoch, set forth in the Book of Enoch, which presumably Luke knew (1 Enoch 10:11-12 (Oxford, 1995; Crane, 1926. Bauckham, Richard {2004}, Jude and Relatives of Jesus in the Early Church, London: T&T Clark International, pgs. 315-373.). However, not everybody agrees. For instance, Irenaeus counts only seventy-two generations from Adam.[45]

Luke's qualification of "as was supposed" expediently avoids stating that Jesus was actually a son of Joseph. This expediency can be explained by his affirmation of the Virgin birth. Early Church scholars, such as John of Damascus, assert the view that "as was supposed" of Joseph regards Luke as calling Jesus the son of Eli/Heli, the maternal grandfather of Jesus, tracing the lineage through Mary.[46] The author concurs with this conclusion: the lineage was traced through Heli/Eli, the maternal grandfather of Mary, and this view can be explained, he believes, in terms of the law of levirate (Deut. 25:5-6; see also Table 4 in Appendix D).

Hence, we can surmise that both Matthew and Luke have affirmed that Joseph was a descendant of David. But, while Matthew derives him from David through his son Solomon, Luke derives him through Nathan, David's older son. This indicates that both parents are from the Davidic tribe of Judah.

The following is a quote from Damascene, where he explains the lineage of Joseph through Heli, the maternal grandfather (see also Table 4 in Appendix D):

---

[42] "Matthew 18:21-22" (Wikipedia, 2020) *The International Bible Society*, Retrieved [Online] from (http://www.biblica.com/bible/?osis=niv:Matthew.18:21-18:22bid Matthew

[43] Crane, 1926

[44] "Genesis 4:24" (Wikipedia, 2020) *The International Bible Society*, Retrieved [Online] from (http://www.biblica.com/bible/?osis=Genesis.4:24-4:24).

[45] Schaff, Philip (1882), The Gospel According to Matthew, New York: Charles Scribner's sons, pg. 4-5

[46] Schaff, Philip (1882), The Gospel According to Matthew, New York: Charles Scribner's sons, pg. 4-5

"…Born then of the line of Nathan, the son of David, Levi begat Melchi and Panther: Panther begat Barpanther, so-called. This Barpanther begat Joachim: Joachim begat the Holy Mother of God. And of the line of Solomon, the son of David, Matthan had a wife of whom he begat Jacob. Now on the death of Matthan, Melchi, of the tribe of Nathan, the son of Levi and brother of Panther, married the wife of Matthan, Jacob's mother, of whom he begat Heli of the tribe of Nathan. Therefore, Jacob and Heli became brothers on tile mother's side, Jacob being of the tribe of Solomon and Heli of the tribe of Nathan. Then Heli of the tribe of Nathan died childless, and Jacob, his brother, of the tribe of Solomon, took his wife and raised up seed to his brother and begat Joseph. Joseph, therefore, is by nature the son of Jacob, of the line of Solomon, but by law, he is the son of Heli of the line of Nathan."[47]

Joachim married the revered and praiseworthy Anna, but being "barren . . . this Anna by supplication and promise from God bare the Mother of God so that she might not even in this be behind the matrons of fame." Now we know the woman involved in the levirate marriage detailed above; she was Estha/Hazibah (see Table 4 in Appendix D). Sextus Julius Africanus, in his third-century *Epistle to Aristides*, concurs with Damascene's explanation above of Joseph's birth through a levirate marriage; he explained it this way: "Matthan, a descendant of Solomon, begat Jacob. After the death of Matthan, Melki," (Melchi a papponymic naming, which could be corrected to Matthat after his grandfather, so Melchi and Matthat could be the same person) "a descendant of Nathan, begat Heli by the same woman" (Estha/Hezibah). "Therefore, Heli and Jacob must be uterine brothers. Heli died childlessl; Jacob raised up his seed by begetting Joseph, who was his son according to the flesh, and Heli's son according to the law. So, we can say that Joseph was the son of them both."

---

[47] Damascene, An Exact Exposition of the Orthodox Faith; Book 1v chapter X1V: Concerning our Lord's genealogy and concerning the holy mother of God.

Patrilineage of Jesus Christ according to Luke 3:23-38

GOD				
1. Adam	17. Ragau	33. Jesse	49. Er	65. Esli
2. Seth	18. Saruch	34. David	50. Elmodam	66. Naum
3. Enos	19. Nachor	35. Nathan	51. Cosam	67. Amos
4. Cainan	20. Thara/ Terah	36. Mattatha	52. Addi	68. Mattathias
5. Maleleel	21. Abraham	37. Menan	53.Melchi	69. Josseph
6. Jared	22. Isaac	38. Melea	54. Neri	70.Jannai
7. Enoch	23. Jacob	39. Eliakim	55. Salathiel	71. Melchi
8. Mathusala	24. Judah	40. Jonam	56. Zorobabel	72. Levi
9. Lamech	25. Phares/ Perez	41. Joseph	57. Rhesa	73. Matthat
10. Noah	26. Esrom/ Hezron	42. Judah	58. Joannan	74. Heli
11. Shem	27. Aram/Ram	43. Simeon	59. Juda/Joda	75. Joseph
12. Arphaxad	28. Amminadab	44. Levi	60. Joseph	76. Jesus
13. Cainan	29. Naasson/ Nahshon	45. Matthat	61. Semei	
14. Shelah	30. Salmon	46. Jorim	62. Mattathias	
15. Heber	31. Boaz	47. Eliezer	63.Maath	
16. Phalec	32. Obed	48. Jose	64. Nagge	

Modern scholars tend to see the genealogies as mere theological constructs rather than a factual history of God's redemptive plan for mankind. Their argument is that family pedigrees would not "usually" be available for non-priestly families. Secondly, the differences between the genealogies from David to Joseph are evidence that they were not based on historical, genealogical records.[48] For instance, Raymond E. Brown states that the genealogies "tell us nothing certain about the grandparents of his great-grandparents."[49]

The contradictions between the two genealogies have been used to question the veracity of the Gospel stories since ancient times. This is especially true coming from the Manichaeans (dual philosophy of either good or evil proponents).

Augustine was thus forced not only to respond to the Manichaeans but also to convince himself of the accuracy of the Gospels, which had caused him some consternation as a youth, most specifically concerning Joseph. He explained that Joseph was both a biological/flesh father and an adoptive one by law and that one of the Gospels (Matthew) traces his genealogy through his biological father and Luke through Mary and his legal father. Thus, he observed a parallel between Joseph and Jesus. But, above all, he concurred with Africanus' position.

This author believes and concurs with both Africanus and Augustine that Matthew traced his genealogy of Christ through Joseph. Luke traced his through Mary by way of her maternal grandfather, Heli/Eli (see Table 4 in Appendix D).

This is especially significant given the miraculous birth of the Virgin narrated in the Proto-Gospel of James (not in the Canon): "While sitting under a tree in her garden and crying her heart out to the Lord, an angel of the Lord appeared to her and said, Anna, Anna, the Lord hath heard thy prayer; thou shalt conceive and bring forth, and thy progeny shall be spoken in all the world" (James' Proto-Gospel 4:1).

Joachim was informed of this message by the angel while he was with his shepherds in the wilderness, where he had fasted for forty days and

[48] Johnson, M. D. (1988), The Purpose of the Biblical genealogies (2nd ed.), Cambridge, England: Cambridge University Press, pg. 142, ISBN 978-0-521-35644-2.
[49] Brown, R.E. (1977) *The Birth of the Messiah*, New York, New York: Doubleday Publishiing, pg. 94

nights praying to the Lord for a child. The angel had informed him to "make haste and go hence, for behold, Anna thy wife shall conceive" (4:4). When Anna met him at the gate, she said, "Now I know that the Lord hath greatly blessed me. For behold, I who was a widow am no longer a widow, and I who was barren shall conceive" (4:9-10). The Proto-Gospel of James was widely in use in the ancient time so that it might have been available to both Matthew and Luke.

Park tried to resolve the discrepancy between the two Gospels regarding Joseph's father in the following manner: He argues that Joseph, who became Eli's/Heli's son-in-law by marrying Marry, legally succeeded his genealogy because of the Old Testament laws, which say that if a man does not have a son, his inheritance must be given to his daughters, provided they marry men from their own tribe to protect their inheritance (Numbers 27:1-8; 36:1-12). Hence, Mary received the inheritance of her father, Eli/Heli, because he didn't have a son, and when she married Joseph from the same tribe, he became Heli's legal successor and son.

Park further posits that the Talmud states that Mary was Heli's daughter, and the Sinaitic-Syriac manuscripts "render Luke 2:4 as follows: They [both Joseph and Mary] were of the house and lineage of Judah."[50] Given these observations, the view that Matthew recorded the genealogy through the line of Joseph and Luke recorded his through the line of Mary—a descendant of David in her own right through his son Nathan— is consistent with the content of the Bible. Thus, Christ became heir to the throne of David through both parents as the virgin-born son of Mary.

In view of the above arguments, the contention that the genealogies, especially that of Luke, could not be that of Mary because of the constraints of maternal lineage in the Jewish law is rendered invalid. And the supposition that Jewish law does not accept maternal ancestry inheritance goes against Numbers 27:1-8 and 36:1-12. God commanded Moses to give the daughters of Zelophehad, of the family of Manasseh, Mahlah, Noah, Hoglah, Milcah, and Tirzah, "a possession of an inheritance among their father's brethren; and thou shalt cause the inheritance of their father to pass unto them" (Numbers27:7). The daughters of Zelophehad followed God's commandment: "For Mahlah, Tirzah, and Hoglah, and Milcah, and Noah . . . were married unto their father's brothers' sons: And they

---

[50] Park(2014) The Promise of the Eternal covenant, pg. 141

were married into the families of the sons of Manasseh the son of Joseph, and their inheritance remained in the tribe of the family of their father" (Numbers 36:11-12).

It's been questioned whether or not the levirate marriages actually happened among uterine brothers, which is expressly disallowed in the Halakhah. Anthony Maas, a Jesuit theologian, posits that the question asked of Jesus about a woman who had seven levirate husbands might suggest that the law was either well alive or, we can surmise, obsolete.[51]

Part of our knowledge of Mary's genealogy was recorded in the Doctrina Jacobi, written in 634 A.D. by a Tiberian rabbi while trying to mock Christians of their veneration of Mary in these terms:

> *Why do Christians extol Mary, calling her nobler than the Cherubim, incomparably greater than the Seraphim, raised above the heavens. Purer than the very rays of the sun? For she was a woman of the race of David, born to Anna, her mother, and Joachim her father, who was the son of Panther. Panther and Melchi were brothers, sons of Levi; of the stock of Nathan, whose father was David of the tribe of Judah.*[52]

John of Damascus and others, a century later, report similar information with the correction of inserting an extra generation, Barpanther (Aramaic for "Son of Panther"). Thus, it is clear from the supporting statement above that it was known even in ancient times that Mary belongs to the tribe of Judah.

---

[51] Maas, A. "Genealogy (in the Bible)". The Catholic Encyclopedia. vol.6. New York, New York: Robert Appleton Company, 1909. 9 Oct. 2013 retrieved [Online] from (http://www.newadvent.org/cathen/06408a.htm).

[52] Doctrina Jacobi, p. 1.42 (PO 40.67–68 (http://www.patristique.org/IMG/pdf/PO_40_VIII_5.pdf)). Translated in part by Williams, A. Lukyn (1935), Adversus Judaeos: a bird's-eye view of Christian apologiae until the Renaissance (https://books.google.com/?id=6m43AAAAIAAJ&pg=PA155), Cambridge University Press, pp. 155–156, OCLC 747771 (http s://www.worldcat.org/oclc/747771)

1 Chronicles 3:19-24: Generations of Zerubbabel's Descendants

Name	Zerubbabel	Hananiah	Shecaniah	Shemaiah	Neariah	Elioenal	Hodaviah
Estimated Period	570 B.C.	545 B.C.	520 B.C.	495 B.C.	470 B.C.	445 B.C.	420 B.C.

*Reckoned with an average of twenty-five years per generation. Courtesy of Park, Abraham (2014) *The Promise of the Eternal Covenant: God's Profound Providence as revealed in the Genealogy of Jesus Christ (The Post-Exilic Period)* North Clarendon, Vermont: Periplus Editions publishers

Shealtiel/Salathiel, Zerubbabel/Zorobobel, and Pedaiah

Another difficulty faced by both Matthew and Luke in their presentation of the two genealogies is that of Zerubbabel and Salathiel/ Shealtiel. The two genealogies converge at Zerubbabel, son of Azi Salathiel/ Shealtiel, but they both differ above and below Zerubbabel.

In the Old Testament, Zerubbabel was presented as a hero who led the Jews to Jerusalem from Babylon in about 520 B.C., during the reign of Cyrus of Persia. He was appointed Governor of Judah and rebuilt the Temple. In 1 Chronicles 3:19, his descendants were traced for several generations, and he was called the son of Pedaiah (Masoretic text). The Septuagint, on the other hand, gives his father as Shealtiel.[53] The genealogical lists of Jesus in both Matthew 1:1-16 and Luke 3:23-38 find common ground in Salathiel and Zerubbabel.[54]

Rhesa, named in Luke 3:27 as the son of Zerubbabel, has been said to be an Aramaic word for "head" or "prince," and it is not found in the Matthean genealogies or the Chronicler's genealogies. He also does not appear among the descendants of Zerubbabel listed in 1 Chronicle 3:19-24. 1 Chronicle 3:19-20 listed the sons of Pedaiah as Zerubbabel and Shimei. The sons of Zerubbabel were Meshullam and Hananiah; Shelomith was their sister. There were also Hashubah, Ohel, Berechiah, Hasadiah, and Jushub-hesed.

Since Zerubbabel was considered the rightful heir in Babylon to his grandfather, Jeconiah/Jehoiachin, the name listed in Matthew 1:1-16, Abiud (not listed among his sons in 1 Chronicles 3:19-20), is supposed to be an heir, even though his name never appeared among Zerubbabel's sons, but he might have been Zerubbabel's youngest son.[55]

Park presents a different argument regarding the appearance of Abiud in the genealogies of Jesus Christ.[56] He observed that, in Hebrew, Abiud means "father," "majesty," or "glory." Thus, it means "Father of glory," "Father is glory," "Father of majesty," or "Father is majesty."

---

[53] We've explored previously why this could be.

[54] Hindson (2013), 3:19, pg. 645

[55] Park (2014); Ibid pg. 102; Crane, 1926. pg. 118-119

[56] Ibid, pg. 117, 164-165

Interestingly, Park observed that other descendants of Zerubbabel, Hodaiah/Hodaviah, has a name with the same meaning (1 Chronicles 3:24). He is listed in 1 Chronicles 3 as the last generation among the descendants of Zerubbabel, whereas Jesus Christ's genealogy in Matthew 3: 13 lists Abiud/Abihud after Zerubbabel.

Since Abiud/Abihud and Hodaiah/Hodaviah have the same meaning to their names, is it possible that the two could be the same person? Park surmises the answer is yes. His conclusion is based on 1 Chronicle 3:19-24, where records of seven generations are given in the line of Zerubbabel: Hananiah, Shecaniah, Shemaiah, Neriah, Elioenai, and Hodaviah.

Given that a generation is given as an average spanning twenty-five years, Hodaviah is presumed to have lived around 420 BC (see Table 3 in Appendix C). This is when the book of Chronicles is presumed to have been written by its probable author, Prophet Ezra.[57] [58] [59]

Hodaviah had six other younger siblings, including Eliashib, Pelaiah, Akkub, Johanan, Delaiah, and Anani, the last of whom was born at the end of the fifth century B.C. (that is, born in the 400s B.C.), at the close of the Old Testament.[60] [61]

In view of the above analysis, it's likely that Hodaviah—the successor to Zerubbabel in the Matthean genealogy of Jesus Christ—who carried Zerubbabel's lineage in 1 Chronicle 3, is the same person who resumes the genealogy from where it stops at the end of 1 Chronicle 3. As I've noted, the meaning of Hodaviah is the same as that of Abihud/Abiud, who succeeds Zerubbabel in the Matthean genealogy.

Given all these facts, there's a strong possibility that the two are one and the same person; both Hervey and Matthew miller, in his discussion

---

[57] Park (2014); Ibid, pg. 165

[58] Hindson (2013)

[59] The Church of Jesus Christ of Latter-Day Saints (Wikipedia, 2020) *Introduction to the Book of 1 King*pg. 733 Retrieved [online] from https://www.churchofjesuschrist.org/study/manual/old-testament-seminary-teacher-manual/introduction-to-the-book-of-1-Kings?lang=eng

[60] Hindson, 2013, 3:10-24, pg. 645

[61] Park (2014); Ibid, pg.165

on the omitted generations after Zerubbabel in Bengel, seem to concur.[62] [63] Either Abihud and Hodaviah are a papponymic naming, referring to the same person, or a clerical error was made because nowhere in the genealogy listed in 1 Chronicle 3 was Abihud mentioned as Zerubbabel's son. There are likely more than five generations between him and Zerubbabel (see Table 3 in Appendix C).

Park also argued that the Zerubbabel and Shealtiel/Salathiel in Matthew (see Table 1 in Appendix A) might be different from the ones in Luke (see Table 2 in Appendix B). His argument is based on the calculation that the Zerubbabel in Matthew was born around 570 B.C. If he is the same person as in Luke, he should also be born in 570 B.C. This means there is a span of 470 years between David and Zerubbabel (David's birth minus Zerubbabel's, 1040 - 570 B.C.) through the line of Nathan in the Lukan genealogy.

There are 22 generations in this 470-year period in the Lukan genealogy (see Table 2 in Appendix B). He argues there is an average interval of 21 years between each generation (470 ÷22). Under a similar premise, he observes, there would be an interval of some 566 years (Zerubbabel's birth date minus Christ's, 570 – 4 B.C.) from Zerubbabel to Jesus Christ in Luke 3 genealogy through Nathan.

Since there are 20 generations (see Table 2 in Appendix B), the average span between each generation would be 28 years (566÷20). In his view, the 21-year average from David to Zerubbabel in the Lukan genealogy and the 28-year average from Zerubbabel to Jesus Christ in the same genealogy is too great. It is significant, even though no test of significance was performed.

From these statistics, he concludes that the Zerubbabel in the Lukan genealogy is not the same person as the one in the Matthean genealogy. However, it seems to me that Park overlooks the fact that generational averages may vary, sometimes even widely, due to some factors, such as periods of peace instead of war, general health awareness in dieting, advancement in medicine for combating pandemics, and society's general prosperity, etc.

---

[62] Lord A. C. Hervey, The Genealogies of Our LORD and savior Jesus Christ (Cambridge: Macmillan and Co., 1853), 123

[63] J. A. Bengel, Gnomon of the New Testament, vol. 1 (Philadelphia: Smith, English, and Co.1860), 87.

A Lukan (3:23-38) Levirate Marriage Family Tree of
the Davidic Line through Solomon and Nathan

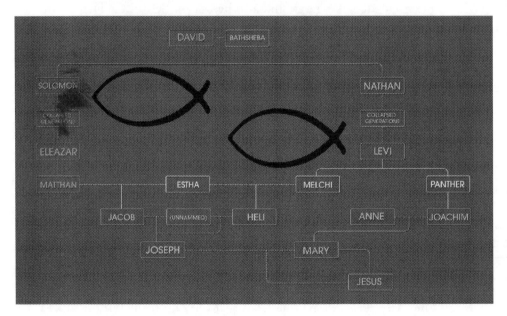

Adopted and greatly modified from "Caffeine for masses": http://
caffeine4masses.blogspot.com/2013/12/

Park goes on to observe that in the Lukan genealogy (see Table 2 in Appendix B), the time span from David to Jesus Christ is 1,036 years (David's birth date minus Christ's, 1040 - 4 B.C.), a total of 42 generations. Thus, he finds the average span of years between generations to be 24.7 (1036 ÷ 42), a number he argues is close to 25, which is traditionally measured as a generation. From this, he concludes there are no generational omissions in the Lukan genealogy corresponding to the second and third periods of the Matthean genealogy.

Applying the average generational span of 24.7 years to the 22 generations between David and Zerubbabel in the Lukan genealogy, Park concludes that Zerubbabel existed 543 years (24.7 x 22) after David. This means Zerubbabel must have been born in 497 B.C. (1040 B.C. - 543 years). Therefore, Park (2014) surmises the two different birth dates for Zerubbabel indicate the one in the Matthean genealogy (born circa 570 B.C.) and the one in the Lukan genealogy (born circa 497 B.C.). Another conclusion Park arrives at is that Shealtiel/Salathiel and Zerubbabel in the Lukan genealogy must have lived 73 years (that is, 570–497 B.C.), or at least three generations, after the ones in the Matthean genealogy. Based on the above calculations, Park concluded there might be up to seven generations omitted between Abiud/Abihud and Jesus Christ in the third period of the Matthean genealogy. This is based on the assumption that we know the birth date of Zerubbabel for certain. We know that King David was born in 1040 B.C. and began his reign at the age of 30 (2. Samuel 5:4), in 1010 B.C., but dates surrounding Zerubbabel are an estimate.[64] Given estimate errors, making such a sweeping conclusion based on uncertain data isn't objectively valid.

Thus far, we have shown the omissions in the third period of the Matthean genealogy: between Josiah and Jeconiah/Jehoiachin and Zedekiah immediately after Jehoiachin. Accordingly, we have presented a situation whereby five generations (Hananiah, Shecaniah, Shemaiah, Neariah, and Elioenai) seemed to be omitted between Zerubbabel and Abiud. We have also indicated the seven generations that might have been

---

[64] Park (2014), pg. 166 - "Since Zerubbabel in Matthew was born around 570 B.C., ... we assume that..." See also, Zerubbabel – Wikipedia, 2020 (Wikipedia, 2020), 3rd Exilarch at *Geni.com* claims birthday is 566 B.C. and death 510 B.C.

omitted between Jesus Christ and Abiud, but we cannot know their names (see Table 3 in Appendix C).

The example of Christ presented in the letter to the Hebrews[65] is that of Melchizedek, the King of Salem ("King of peace"), who was featured in the Old Testament as a priest to Abraham and "The priest of the Most High God" after a successful war victory (Genesis 14:18-20). In the Genesis story, it is said that he gave Abraham bread and wine after his return from a victorious battle. Abraham gave him his tithe from this bounty (Genesis 14:20).

The unique historical story of Melchizedek told in Genesis 14:18-19 is that he had no parents (nobody knew them, at least), but he was still righteous. He had "neither beginning of days nor end of life" and was "made like the son of God" (Heb. 7:3). Melchizedek has been viewed as "a priest perpetually" even though he was not included in the genealogy of the Levites as a member of the priesthood (Heb. 7:3, 6). Jesus, like Melchizedek, He is the "Eternal God who is without genealogy from the beginning, and the High Priest according to the power of an indestructible life."/who is made, not after the law of a carnal commandment, but after the power of an endless life [66] Similarly, the priesthood of Jesus was "according to the order of Melchizedek whose genealogy is not traced from the Levites."[67]

Some have posited that the Matthean genealogy seems to be traced through Joseph (Matt 1:1-16) and that the Lukan (Luke 3:23-38) is traced through Mary, but there are those who believe both Evangelists trace the

---

[65] Epistle to the Hebrews, (Wikipedia, 2020) Wikipedia, 2020- The author of Hebrews has been unknown since the second century. Paul was accepted as the author in the East from the early second century to the third, but he was rejected in the West, where the Epistle was known from earlier times. In fact, since the second century, a great ancient Christian scholar, Origen of Alexandria, had to concede by saying, "Only God truly knows who the author of this epistle is" (Introduction of the Epistle to the Hebrews, KJV, second edition). The search for authorship had ranged from St. Paul to Barnabas and Silas to Apollos, an Alexandrian Jew. Those who oppose Paul's authorship observe what the author said about himself in Hebrews 2:3: that his knowledge of "Christ was secondhand." By contrast, they point out that Paul himself has always "declared his apostleship and message were directly from Jesus Christ," as seen in Galatians 1:1; 12

[66] Heb. 7:16 (NASB; Hindson, 2013, Heb. 7:16); See Park A. 2014, pg. 81

[67] Heb. 7:6 (NASB); Park A. Ibid.

genealogies through Joseph.[68] This author concurs with the former view, posited by Africanus et al., by Park, and by Hindson (2013)(see Table 4 in Appendix D).[69]

Psalm 132:11-12 states, "The LORD hath sworn in truth unto David; he will not turn from it; of the fruits of thy body will I set upon thy throne. If thy children will keep my covenant and my testimony that I shall teach them, their children shall also sit upon thy throne forevermore." In this sense, Mary had to be physically descended from David in order for the prophecies to be fulfilled. As I argued earlier, I believe that was the case: Mary belonged to the Davidic line of Judah through David's elder son Nathan. Of great interest are the circumstances of her miraculous birth, narrated in the Proto-Gospel of James and explored previously.

Indeed, it's a mystery that the name of Jesus Christ would be linked to a genealogy of mortals, according to flesh in which life and death repeat, even though we know he had no beginning and is everlasting. It is only through God's manifestation of his plan that we are able to understand his great and mysterious administration hidden in the genealogies.

The Epistle to the Hebrews testifies that Jesus was "another priest," who came "according to the order of Melchizedek," whose priesthood excels above all (7:11). Unlike the Levitical priests, he's forever and immutable: "He is the eternal God who is without genealogy from the beginning and the high priest according to the power of an indestructible life" (Heb. 7:16).[70] In John 8:5, 51-58, Jesus shows his deity/divine beginning by telling the Jews who were questioning who he was, "If a man keeps my saying, he shall never see death" (8:51). They became agitated and questioned whether he was more significant than their father, Abraham. He answered, "Your father Abraham rejoiced to see my day: and he saw it, and was glad" (John 8:56). When they challenged his youthfulness, he said to them, "Before Abraham was, *I am*" (John 8:58, emphasis added). *Ego eimi* is the original means "That is eternal."

---

[68] "Genealogy of Jesus", *Wikipedia, 2020* November 28, Wikipedia, 2020, Retrieved [Online] from (https://en.Wikipedia, 2020.org/wiki/genealogy of Jesus, pg. 6/21

[69] Hindson (2013), *K.J.V., Study Bible*, second edition, text and annotation 1:1, 2, pg. 1364

[70] Ibid

CHAPTER IX

OMISSIONS

First- and Second-Period Omissions

Ram/Aram and Amminadab

The omissions clearly in the first period of the genealogy of Jesus Christ in both Matthew (1:16) and Luke (3:23-38) each include a large chunk of generations in the 430-year bondage in Egypt, especially the time between Aram/Ram and Amminadab, who were listed in Ruth 4:19, Matthew 1:3-4, and 1 Chronicle 2:9-10. Perez's son Hezron/Esrom was one of the seventy who traveled to Egypt with Jacob, as shown in Genesis 46:12. According to Park, this indicates that Hezron and his son Ram/Aram, the second born to him by his first wife, lived during the early part of the 430-year period in Egypt (1 Chronicles 2:9).[71] [72]In this case, argues Park, there wasn't any omission. However, Amminadab, listed as Ram's son in Mathew 1:1-4, lived toward the end of the 430-year bondage in Egypt.

His daughter Elisheba (Naashon's sister) married Aaron, a leader during the wilderness journey (Ex. 6:23). Amminadab, therefore, was Aaron's father-in-law. Naashon, Amminadab's son, was also a leader as a household head of the family of Judah during the same era in the wilderness sojourn (Numbers 1:7; 2:3; 1 Chronicles 2:10). Thus, while Hezron/Esrom and Ram/Aram lived in the early part of the period of slavery, Amminadab and Nahshon/Nasson lived close to the end of the 430-year period.

---

[71] Park (2014), pg. 75, Ruth 4:19
[72] Crane (1926). Matthew 1:3-4, 1Chronicles 2:9-10

Kings Omitted in the Second Period in Matthew 1:1-16

OLD TESTAMENT 1 Chronicles 3; Appro. Reign Period*		MATTHEW 1:1-17	Luke 3:23-38
David	1010–970 BC	David	David
Solomon /Jedidiah	970–930BC	Solomon	Nathan
Rehoboam*	CR 931–914 BC	Rehoboam	Mattatha
Abijah/Abijam/Abia*	913–911	Abia	Menna
Asa	910–869 BC	Asaph	Melea
Jehoshaphat*	872–847 BC	Josaphat	Eliakim
Joram/Jehoram *	852–841 BC	Joram	Jonam
Ahaziah/Jehoahaz	841 BC	Omitted	Joseph
Athaliah (Jehoram's wife)	841–835 BC	Omitted	Omitted
Joash	835–796BC	Omitted	Judah
Amaziah*	796–767 BC	Omitted	Simeon
Azariah/Uzziah*	791–739 BC	Ozias	Levi
Jotham*	752–736	Jotham	Matthat
Ahaz*	743 BC; 736–720 BC	Achaz	Jorim
Hezekiah*	729/8–699/8 BC	Ezekias	Eliezer
Manasseh	698–643 BC	Manasses	Joshua
Amon	642–640 BC	Amos	Er
Josiah	640–609 BC	Josiah	Elmadam
Jehoahaz/Shallum	609 BC	Omitted	Cosam
Jehoiakim/Eliakim	609–598 BC	Third period	Addi
Jeconiah/Jehoiachin	598 BC	Omission	Melchi
Jechonias/Jehoiachin/ Coniah		---------------	Neri
Zedekiah (last Kings of Judah)	597–586 BC	Jechonias	Shealtiel
Deported to Babylon by Nebuchadnezzar ---------- ----------- ----------------------		---------------	Zerubbabel
- ----------- ----------------------------		Salathiel	Rhesa
------- ---------------------------- ---------------		Zerubbabel	Joanan
---------- -------- ----------------------		---------------	Joda
---------- -------- ----------------------		---------------	Josech
---------------- ----------- ----------------------		---------------	Semein

95

-----	-----	Mattathias
-----	-----	Maath
-----	-----	Naggai
-----	-----	Esli
-----	-----	Nahum
-----	-----	
-----	-----	Amos
-----	Abiud	Mattathias
-----	Eliakim	Joseph
-----	Azor	Jannai
-----	Zadok	Melchi
-----	Achim	Levi
-----	Eliud	Matthat
-----	Eleazar	Heli
-----	Mathan	Joseph
-----	Jacob	Jesus
-----	Joseph	
-----	Jesus	

*CR: Co-regency rule

This, Park argues, clearly shows some omission between Aram/Ram with Amminadab (namely, how could he be the elder of the tribe of Judah if his father was still there?).[73] This seems to show a period of complete omission during the slavery era. It seems God, in his divine work, has removed from the genealogy of his Son the period of slavery in a gentile country, under tyrannous gentile Kings.

Salmon and Boaz

There is also an omission between Salmon, the father of Boaz, and Boaz (a 300-year period), while both were listed in Ruth 4:21, Crane, 1926. Matthew 1:1-5, and 1 Chronicle 2:11-12.[74] Salmon, who married Rahab/Rachab (the Jericho harlot) when Israel entered Canaan, lived during the early conquest of Canaan and, therefore, both lived at the same time. However, Boaz, who married Ruth and is recorded as Salmon's son, lived at the end of the dark period of the Judges (Park, A. 2014, pg.76).

The Bible testifies that there are no gaps between Boaz, Obed, Jesse, and David (Ruth 4:13-22). This means Obed is David's grandfather (Ruth 4:13-17, 21-22). David was born circa 1040 B.C., began his reign at the age of 30, and ruled from 1010–970 B.C. (2 Samuel 5:4).[75] If he was born in 1040 B.C. and a generation is between 25–30 years, it can be estimated that Obed was born around 1100–1090 B.C., which coincides with Judge Jephthah (1104–1099 B.C.), who condemned as unjustified the invasion of the Ammonites after Israel had occupied the land for 300 years (Judg. 11:26).

This means about three hundred years plus sixteen years of the conquest of Canaan were omitted during the spiritually dark period of the Judges between Salmon and Boaz (judg.2:7-10; 17:16. 21:25).[76] [77] The period of the Judges is said to have been evil and decadent, where "there was no King in Israel" (Judg. 17:6, 21-25). Thus, God entirely omitted this

---

[73] ibid; Exo. 6:23; Numbers1:7; 2:3; 1 Chronicles 2:10
[74] Reference Judges 11:26
[75] Hindson, 2013, *Doctrinal footnote*, 17:12, pg. 473.
[76] Park (2014), pg. 158
[77] Crane (1926)

three-hundred-year period of spiritual decadence and darkness from the genealogy of his Son as well (Judg. 2:7-10; 17:6; 21:25).

The Three Kings Omitted in the Second Period Between Joram and Uzziah/Azariah and Athaliah

Chronologically, the second period of Jesus Christ's genealogy starts with the beginning of David's reign in Jerusalem in 1003 B.C., and it ends with Jeconiah's deportation to Babylon in 597 B.C. by Nebuchadnezzar, spanning 406 years.[78] [79] The three Kings omitted are between Joram and Uzziah/Azariah (Matthew 1:18). However, according to the genealogy in Chronicles 3, generations have been omitted between Joram and Uzziah/Azariah (2 Kings 14:21; 2 Chronicles 26:1; see also Table 5 in Appendix E).

This list excludes Athaliah, the daughter of Ahab and Jezebel, who ruled after her son Ahaziah was killed. Besides Athaliah, Kings omitted include Ahaziah, Joash, and Amaziah (see Table 5 in Appendix E). This means there are actually four omitted in the second period of the genealogy of Christ as presented in Matthew 1:1-16 if we then include the brutal six-year reign of Athaliah (2 Kings 11:3; 2 Chronicles 22:12).

The single thread tying all three Kings together is their descendant through Athaliah, who tried to annihilate all the Davidic royal princes after the death of her son Ahaziah (2 King 11:1; 2 Chronicles 22:10). All three Kings are three generations (Ahaziah, Joash, and Amaziah) of Athaliah's descendants. The second reason they were all omitted is they were all evil Kings who introduced the worship of idols in Judah (2 King 8:27; 2 Chronicles 22:3). Worst of all, they all experienced wretched deaths. The omission of these three Kings demonstrates God's redemptive administration of justice to all the evil powers that tried to quench the lamp of the divine covenant prophesied through the ages.

The Four Women

The inclusion of the four women and men who produced seed for the genealogy of Christ is a clear and powerful demonstration to us of God's

---

[78] Hindson, 2013, (1003-597) = 406
[79] Park (2014), pg. 158.

eternal plan for the inclusion of gentiles in his salvation plan—and of his readiness not to remember our sins and iniquity when we ask for his grace. These are Judah and Tamar (the Canaanite who seduced Judah, her father-in-law) Salmon and Rahab (or Rachab, the Jericho harlot who colluded with Joshua's spies), Boaz and Ruth (the Moabite who married Naomi's son and returned with her to Judea), and David and Bathsheba[80] (the daughter of Eliam and the wife of Uriah, the Hittite).

Third Period Omissions

Chronologically, the third period of Jesus Christ's genealogy spans some 593 years and covers 14 generations from the Israelite deportation (to Babylon during the reign of Jeconiah/Jehoiachin in 597 B.C.) to the birth of Christ around 4 B.C. The omissions include three or four Kings; if we include Athaliah around the period of deportation to Babylon, these are Jehoahaz and Jehoiakim, who came after Josiah and Jeconiah (see Tables 5 (in Appendix E) and 6 (in Appendix F), and Zedekiah, who came after Jehoiakim.

Comparison of Matthean and Lukan genealogies

As we've noted, the genealogy of Matthew diverges from Luke's after David (see Tables 2 and 3).[81] In the Matthean genealogy, there are 27 generations from Solomon to Jesus Christ, while Luke's has 42 generations corresponding to the same period, a difference of 15 generations or 375 years (25x15; see Tables 1 (in Appendix A) and 2 (in Appendix B).

This difference tells us two things. One, either Luke shortened the traditional span of a generation (25–30 years), or Matthew underestimated (or collapsed) intervening generations. Some scholars suggest that the

---

[80] As noted previously, theirs was an adulterous relationship. Psalm 51 has been recognized as David's solemn repentance after his sin with Bathsheba. This teaches us that those who have failed and repented of their sin can receive God's grace and be restored to God's service.

[81] Narrative citation Dr. Ayuba Mshelia (Wikipedia, 2020) (Personal communication) - To recap, the genealogy of Mathew continues with Solomon, David's younger son, while Luke's continues with Nathan, another of David's sons, older than Solomon.

two genealogies also differ in terms of through whom they trace their lineages; Park, for instance, thinks Matthew's is through Joseph and Luke's through Mary.[82] This author concurs with him as well as with the ancient traditional Christian scholars.[83] The assertion that both Evangelists traced their lineages through Joseph remains murky and questionable (see Table 5 in Appendix E).

The genealogy in 1 Chronicle is recorded to assure the returning captives from Babylon that they remain God's chosen people and that the history of God's "elect is perpetual."[53] In 1 Chronicle 3, the last genealogy of all the descendants of Zerubbabel was listed: Hananiah, Shecaniah, Shemaiah, Neriah, Elioenai, and Hodaviah; it excludes Abiud/Abihud, who appears after Zerubbabel in the Matthean genealogy as his son (1 Chronicles 3:19-24; Matthew 1:3).

In 1 Chronicles 3:22-24, Shemaiah—the son of Shechaniah—is said to have had six sons, but only five are listed by name: Hattush, Igeal, Bamaiah, Neariah, and Shaphat. The sons of Neariah were three: Elioenai, Hezekiah, and Azrikam. The sons of Elioenai were Hodaiah/Hodaviah,[84] Eliashib, Pelaiah, Akkub, Johanan, Dalaiah, and Anani (born at the end of the fifth century B.C., at the close of the Old Testament Canon, in the early 400s B.C.).[85]

Three Kings Omitted

Matthew 1:11 states that "Josiah became the father of Jeconiah and his brothers, at the time of the deportation to Babylon," but—according to the Chronicler's genealogy—Jeconiah wasn't Josiah's son; he was Jehoiakim's (2 Kings 24:6; 2 Chronicles 36:8). This would make him Josiah's grandson instead. Thus, three Kings are omitted in the genealogy of Jesus Christ around the Babylonian deportation. Josiah had four sons (see Table 5 in Appendix E). Johanan was the first, followed by Jehoiakim/Eliakim, Zedekiah/Mattaniah, and Shallum/Jehoahaz. Jehoiakim's mother was

---

[82] Park (2014), pg. 141

[83] Such as Africanus, Eusebius (Church History, Life of Constantine; VII), and Damascene (Book IV, Chapter XIV).

[84] Presumed to have lived around 420 BC.

[85] Hindson (2013), 3;10-24, pg. 645.

Zebidah (daughter of Pedaiah of Rumah. 2 King 23:36), and the mother of Zedekiah and Jehoahaz/Shallum was Hamutal (daughter of Jeremiah of Libnah, 2 King 23:31; 24:18). Order of ascension to the throne, however, differs from the order of birth (1 Chronicles 3:15; see also Table 6 in Appendix F). According to the records available, out of all of Josiah's children, only Johanan never became King (see Table 6 in Appendix F).

Jehoahaz/Shallum ("The Lord has grasped")

The omissions occurring in the third period of the genealogy of Christ in the Matthean presentation include Jehoahaz/Shallum, Jehoiakim/Eliakim, and Zedekiah/Mattaniah (see Table 5 in Appendix E).

Jehoahaz/Shallum was the youngest of Josiah's four children.[86] He maneuvered his way—through popular support and brutal abilities—to become King of Judah (Jeremiah 22:11-12). Even though he wasn't the oldest, he was the first to become King after the death of his father, Josiah, given his popularity with the people (see Table 4 in Appendix D). However, he turned out to be an evil and brutal King—as brutal as a lion. In short, "he did evil in the sight of the Lord, according to all that his fathers had done" (2 Kings 23:32).

Pharaoh Neco/Necho of Egypt (who took over from his father, Psammatichus I, in 609 B.C.) fought and defeated Judah at Megiddo. He had Jehoahaz/Shallum carried away to Egypt by hooks. Jehoahaz died there as a captive (2 King 23:34; 2 Chronicles 36:4). Jehoahaz trusted his own abilities, not God. He rejected living a life that depended upon God and, instead, relied on his own power. In the end, he was subjected to the shame of being recorded last in the Chronicler's genealogies even though he was the first to become a king among his brothers (1 Chronicles 3:15; see also Table 6 in Appendix F).

Table 6 (in Appendix F) shows that the genealogy in 1 Chronicles 3:15 was not recorded according to birth order. Rather, Zedekiah and

---

[86] Johanan (Wikipedia, 2020) Wikipedia, 2020, retrieved [Online] from https://en.Wikipedia, 2020.org/wiki/Johanan (High Priest), Johanan was the first, Eliakim/Jehoiakim the second, and Zedekiah/Mattaniah the third.

Jehoahaz[87] are recorded together. One of the reasons why the youngest brother, Zedekiah/Mattaniah, was recorded first in 1 Chronicle 3:15 and 2 Kings 23:30 is likely because of Jehoahaz's short and brutal reign, which lasted only three months. During this short period, he did evil in the sight of the Lord, according to all that his fathers had done.

Jehoiakim/Eliakim was then made King in Jehoahaz's place.[88] Jehoahaz's Kinship seems to have been denied or downplayed by the Chronicler, who said, "Jehoiakim succeeded Josiah" (2 King 23:34). Jehoahaz died a miserable death in Egypt as a captive—just as it was prophesied by Jeremiah:

> *Weep ye not for the dead, neither bemoan him: but weep sore for him that goeth away: for he shall return no more, nor see his native country.*

> *For thus saith the Lord touching Shallum the son of Josiah King of Judah, which reigned instead of Josiah his father, which went forth out of this place; He shall not return thither any more:*

> *But he shall die in the place whither they have led him captive, and shall see this land no more.*
> Jeremiah 22:10-12

Jehoiakim/Eliakim ("The Lord Raises up; God raises up")

Jehoiakim was the eighteenth King of Judah. His original name was Eliakim, but Pharaoh Necho changed it to Jehoiakim to show Judah's subordination to Egypt. He was a tyrant full of greed (2 Kings 23:27; 2 Chronicles 36:5). He exacted silver and gold from the people to pay tribute

---

[87] Hindson (2013) - Brothers with the same mother, Hamutal; see 2 Kings 23:31; 24:18.

[88] Ibid - Eliakim/Jehoiakim the son of Zebudah, the daughter of Pedaiah of Rumah, was made King in place of Jehoahaz by Pharaoh-nechoh of Egypt (2 Kings 23:34-24:1-4). Pharaoh-nechoh changed his name from Eliakim to Jehoiakim. Nevertheless, Jehoiakim's anti-Babylonian policies resulted in him being bound in chains to Babylon by Nebuchadnezzar (2 Kings 24:1-4; 2 Chronicles 36:5-7).

to Pharaoh Necho. He ruled with abandoned coercion in order to collect surplus taxes for the tribute to Egypt, and he used the surplus for his personal ambitions, building an extravagant palace for himself.

Jehoiakim was criticized by Jeremiah for his naked ambition and vanity in the following terms:

> *That saith, I will build me a wide house and large *chambers, and cutteth him out windows; and it is ceiled with cedar; and painted with vermilion.*

> *Shalt though reign, because *closest thyself in cedar? Did not thy father eat and drink, do judgment and justice, and then it was well with him?*

> *He judged the cause of the poor and needy; then it was well with him: was not this to know me? Saith the Lord.*
> *Jeremiah 22: 14-16*

He also persecuted God's prophet and cut the scroll of God's Word with a scribe's knife before burning it. He killed Uriah and dumped his body in the burial place of the common people (Jeremiah 22:17; 26:23). He made attempts on Jeremiah's life, and he never repented for his evil acts. He was taken by Nebuchadnezzar to Babylon in bronze chains around 602 B.C., but he was released and returned to Jerusalem to rule for another 11 years (until 597 B.C.).

According to tradition, he was killed in line with Jeremiah's prophecy: at the hands of Nebuchadnezzar's servants in the 8th month of 597 BC, and he was thrown out of the city—just as Jeremiah had prophesied years earlier.

Jehoiakim did not depend upon the power of God but, rather, on his own and that of Egypt. He did evil in the sight of the Lord and died a tragic and miserable death when he was only thirty-six years old—just before Nebuchadnezzar entered Jerusalem (2 Chronicles 36:5).

Zedekiah/Mattaniah ("The Lord is righteous; The Lord's gift")

Zedekiah replaced Jeconiah/Jehoiachin to serve as the twentieth and final King of Judah (his real name was Mattaniah, but changed to Zedekiah). Nebuchadnezzar changed it to Zedekiah and made him coregent, and served as a vassal under an oath of allegiance to Nebuchadnezzar). Aside from being Josiah's son, he was Jeconiah's uncle (2 Kings 24:17; Jeremiah 37:1; see also Table 5 in Appendix E). He did evil in the sight of the Lord. But in the ninth year of his reign (588 B.C.), Nebuchadnezzar, King of Babylon, attacked Jerusalem, after he conspired to revolt against Babylon with Egypt's help. Zedekiah became anxious and sought God's assurance through Jeremiah. God, however, told Jeremiah to tell King Zedekiah and the people not to challenge Nebuchadnezzar's mighty army. Jerusalem would be destroyed, and great lives would be lost.

Zedekiah and the people ignored God's prophesy not to resist the Babylonian army (Jeremiah 21:3-10):

> *And unto this people thou shalt say, thus saith the **Lord**; Behold, I set before the way of life, and death.*
>
> *He that abideth in this city shall die by the sword, and by the famine, and by the pestilence: but he that goeth out, and falleth to the Chaldeans that besiege you, he shall live, and his live shall be unto him for a prey."*
> Jeremiah 21:8-9

Zedekiah and the people of Judah ignored God's Prophet and, instead, listened to false prophets' prophesies, which predicted the opposite. Through Prophet Jeremiah, God warned the people of Judah multiple times to surrender to Nebuchadnezzar to live. Meanwhile, false prophets made prophesies contrary to Jeremiah's, thereby causing confusion among the populace.

These false prophets, among whom was Hananiah, tried to incite and drive the true Prophet in to corner: "And it shall come to pass, that the nation and Kingdom which will not serve . . . Nebuchadnezzar . . . Babylon, and will not put their neck under the yoke of the King of Babylon, that nation will I punish . . . with the sword, and with the famine, and with the pestilence, until I have consumed them by his hand" (Jeremiah 27:8).

King Zedekiah and his people refused to "bring [their] necks under the yoke of the King of Babylon, and serve him and his people, and live" (Jeremiah 27:12). In fact, to maximize God's seriousness of the matter, Jeremiah put a wooden yoke around his neck as a symbol of his obedience to God's words.

But the people not only didn't listen to Jeremiah; Hananiah faced Jeremiah and broke the wooden yoke around his neck. The Lord God responded by instructing Jeremiah to tell King Zedekiah and his officials that it would no longer be a wooden yoke. It would be an infernal, iron yoke, meaning that anybody who resisted would die, and the city would be destroyed entirely.

Even after multiple dire warnings, the people resisted God's command. God, therefore, commanded Jeremiah to prophesy the death of Hananiah (since he was one of the chief leaders of the false prophets who were contradicting God's true message). Within a short time, Hananiah died (Jeremiah 28: 17).

It was very hard for the people and their king to surrender without a fight, but that was God's word for them. King Zedekiah did not consider the will of God, but he should have humbly accepted God's word. Instead, he sent an envoy with horses and troops to pharaoh Hophra for help. When the Babylonians heard the Egyptians were on their way, they tactically withdrew and lifted the siege of Jerusalem.

Zedekiah thought he had completely fended off the mighty Babylonian offensive with the Egyptian power. But as soon as the Egyptians withdrew, the Babylonians returned with a vengeance to Judah and besieged the city again. This was during Zedekiah's ninth year as a King

Jeremiah was accused of treason and put in the "stocks" at the upper Benjamin Gate. Despite the obvious sign of decline in security, the people continued to be comforted falsely, arguing that God would never allow Jerusalem to be destroyed. Jeremiah cried even louder for obedience to God's message when the fall and destruction of the city became imminent, but no one listened. Instead, he was thrown into a dungeon by Irijah, the captain of the guards (Jeremiah 37:13). Jeremiah became scared for his life.

But then, unexpectedly, when it was almost too late to ask God for the city to be spared, King Zedekiah sent for Jeremiah. God commanded his prophet to tell King Zedekiah, "thou shalt be delivered into the hand of the King of Babylon" (Jeremiah 37:17).

King Zedekiah was left alone (most of the false prophets went into hiding). Jeremiah pleaded for his innocence, and Zedekiah commanded he be put in the court of the prison (guardhouse) and given daily piece of bread each day out of the baker's street "until all the bread in the city were spent. Thus, Jeremiah remained in the court of the prison" (Jer. 37:21). Even though Zedekiah knew Jeremiah was God's true prophet, he was afraid of his officials and surrendered to their whims: "Behold, he is in your hands, for the King can do nothing against you" (Jeremiah 38:5).

The councilors met and decided to put Jeremiah in the cistern, which was used as a well. However, the one he was thrown into had no water—only mud. Jeremiah sank into the mud, his body and feet buried, and he was left cold and hungry. All Jeremiah received from proclaiming God's true prophesy to Zedekiah and his people were contempt, persecution, humiliation, and mental and physical suffering.

King Nebuchadnezzar besieged the city for two years and six months (from the ninth year of Zedekiah's reign to the eleventh). Jerusalem suffered such untold famine and pestilence that, toward the end of the siege, people even began to practice cannibalism by boiling and eating their own children as prophesied by Jeremiah and confirming the curse Moses pronounced would fall upon Israel should they fail to follow God's commandments (Lam. 4:10; 5:10-23; Jeremiah 19:9; Lev. 26:29; Deut. 28:57; 2 King 6:29).

Jeremiah expressed God's message to the people as follows:

> *And I will make them to eat the flesh of their sons and the flesh of their daughters, and they shall eat every one the flesh of his friend in the siege and straitness (desperation), wherewith their enemies, and they that seek their lives, shall straiten them.*
> *Jeremiah 19:9*

Eventually, God gave them into the hands of the Chaldean army. Jerusalem fell in the eleventh year of King Zedekiah's reign (586 B.C.).

Zedekiah was captured by Nebuchadnezzar's army when he was trying to escape, and he was forced to watch as his own children were brutally butchered in front of him before his eyes were plucked out and he was led into captivity in Babylon (2 King 25:7).

During the first deportation in 605 B.C., the Chaldeans took "some of the vessels of the house of God" (Dan.1:2). Then, during the second deportation in 597 B.C., they carried "all the treasures of the house of the Lord," and "cut in pieces all the vessels of gold which Solomon King of Israel . . . in the Temple of the Lord" (2 Kings 24:13; Jeremiah 52:17-20). The third deportation (in 586 B. C.) is described in 2 Kings 25:13-16:

And the pillars of brass that were in the house of the Lord, and the bases, and the brazen sea that was in the house of the Lord, did the Chaldeans break into pieces and carried the brass of them to Babylon.

The pots, and the shovels, and the snuffers, and the spoons, and all the vessels of brass wherewith they ministered, they took away.

And the firepans, and the bowls, and such things as were of gold, in gold, and of silver, in silver, the captain of the guard took away.

The two pillars, one sea, and the bases which Solomon had made for the house of the Lord, the brass of all these vessels were without weight.

The history of Judah began in 930 B.C. and ended in 586 B.C., lasting a total of 344 years. Each of these three Kings did evil according to all that their fathers had done (2 King 23:32; 24:9). All three did evil in the sight of the Lord, and they never repented. All three put their trust in things and idols instead of in the God of Israel, who freed them from slavery in Egypt.

The Kings Omitted from the Genealogy of Jesus Christ in the Third Period in Matthew 1:1-16

		1	2	3	4
Chronicler's Genealogy (1 Chronicles 3:15)	Josiah	Johanan	Jehoiakim (Eliakim)	Zedekiah (Mattaniah)	Jehoahaz (Shallum)
Order of Birth	Josiah	Johanan	Jehoiakim	Jehoahaz (Shallum)	Zedekiah
Order of accession)	Josiah	Jehoahaz (Shallum)	Jehoiakim (Eliakim)	Jehoiachin (Jeconiah)	Zedekiah (Mattaniah)
Matthean Genealogy (Matthew 1:10-11)	Josiah	Jehoahaz Omitted	Jehoiakim Omitted	Jeconiah Jehoiachin	Zedekiah Omitted

Adopted from Park (2014) with Modifications

CHAPTER X

SUMMARY AND CONCLUSIONS

From our preceding presentation of the brief summaries of each of the individuals that appear in the genealogies of the Son of God in both Matthew 1:1-16 and Luke 3:23-38, we can—with a certain level of confidence—say that they were not perfect men. They were, rather, men with shortcomings who were able and willing to seek and ask for divine forgiveness from the Lord God.

God's divine redemptive plan for history since the world's foundation was always to redeem and forgive his children when they make a mistake and come to him for cleansing and renewal. Take King David and his adulterous relationship with Bathsheba. David grieved and repented because he recognized that his sin had brought the name of God into disrepute.

The seed of King David's son immediately bore the brunt of said sin by becoming grievously ill and dying. However, through David's repentance, God's grace was made abundant, and he allowed Bathsheba to give birth to another son, Solomon or Jedidiah ("Beloved of the Lord"), one through whom the promise of the Davidic covenant would continue.

As I previously mentioned, it is generally believed that Psalm 51 was written sometime after King David's sin. It expresses the sentiment of David being "a man after God's own heart." He wasn't a perfect man, but he was sensitive to sin and willing to acknowledge it the way few people are. In the Psalm, after confessing his guilt, David prayed for inner renewal, and he promised thanksgiving to the almighty God. In the closing verses, he asked God to restore the "joy of [his] salvation."

The message of Psalm 51 is that the Lord God is gracious and merciful, and he will restore to his service those who have failed, even including them in the genealogy of his son.

Another example can be found in Judah. Judah's relationship with Tamar is another failure, but God restored him to prominence through the blessings of his father, Jacob (Israel). He responded with anger when he was told his daughter-in-law was pregnant, saying, "She is with child by whoredom. . .. Bring her forth, and let her be burnt" (Genesis 38:24). However, when Tamar showed him the items she'd taken from him (signet, bracelet, and staff), which belonged to the man by whom she was with child, Judah recognized and acknowledged they were his. He meekly said, "She hath been more righteous than I, because that I gave her not to Shelah my son" (Genesis 38:26). It is the fruit of this pregnancy that produced one of the ancestors (Pharez/Perez; see Tables 1 and 2) mentioned in the genealogy of Jesus Christ.

We know what the Lord God told Moses when Moses asked that the Lord blot his name from "out thy book which thou have written": "Whosoever hath sinned against me, he will I blot out of the book" (Ex. 32:32-33). There has been considerable discussion about the identity of the book. Some have argued it refers to the "Book of Life," in which believers' names are recorded. Some, on the other hand, see it as a "register" of living men with direct reference to present life. A third group argues it refers to the names of those who would enter the Promised Land. Thus, to be blotted out would mean death.

However, given that three thousand people fell on that day, it's possible that it refers to temporal and not eternal life. Furthermore, the Lord God said he "will be gracious to whom I will be gracious, and will shew mercy on whom I will shew mercy" (Ex. 33:19). This message indicates that God, in His divine redemptive plan of administering justice from the foundation of the world, predestined and sanctified his "elect" to be part of his redemptive history of salvation.

In the preceding chapters, I have tried to examine the actions and deeds of the fourteen people who appear in the third period of the Matthean genealogy of Jesus Christ, including the names of those omitted (see Tables 5 and 6). This is especially relevant to the three Kings who reigned around the time of the deportation to Babylon: Jehoahaz/Shallum, Jehoiakim/

Eliakim, and Zedekiah/Mattaniah. At this juncture, we need not repeat their evil deeds or those of their fathers before them.

One sin worth noting, though, is the sin of idolatry. Jeremiah repeatedly warned against idolatrous ways, which would forsake God in favor of worshipping other gods (2 Chronicles 34:25; Jeremiah 1:16; 3:13; 5:19). Nevertheless, people never heeded Jeremiah's message. Worse, they even denied the existence of God and killed some of his prophets (Jeremiah 5:12-13).

God warned Israel of his judgment through three prohibitions given to Jeremiah: to not take a wife or have children to be saved from the calamity to come (Jeremiah 16:1-13). He was also not to enter a house of mourning and not to go to any house of feasting, "to sit with them to eat or drink" ({Jeremiah 16:8}; 16:5-7, 8-9).

But the people sinned by not keeping the Sabbath day and the Sabbatical year (Deut. 15:12-18). Keeping the Sabbath day determines if a person has obeyed or disobeyed the law, determining God's blessings or woes. This is so because the law was given as an eternal symbol to show that it is God who sanctifies his chosen people (Ex. 31:13). The people's failure to keep the Sabbath day was one reason for their deportation to Babylon:

> *Thus, saith the Lord; take heed to yourselves, and bear no burden on the sabbath day, nor bring it in by the gates of Jerusalem; neither carry forth a burden out of your houses on the sabbath day, neither do ye any work, but hallow ye the Sabbath day, as I commanded your fathers. But they obeyed not, neither inclined their ear, but made their neck stiff, that they might not hear, nor receive instruction... If ye diligently hearken unto me . . . to bring in no burden through the gates of the city on the Sabbath day... The men of Judah and the inhabitants of Jerusalem: and this city shall remain forever... But if ye will not hearken unto me to hallow the Sabbath day, and not to bear the burden... Then I will Kindle a fire in the gates thereof, and it shall devour the palaces of Jerusalem, and it shall not be quenched.*
> Jeremiah 17:21-27

The arrogant attitude of the people finally reached a point of no return in the eyes of the Lord, and he declared to Jeremiah, "All this land shall be a desolation, and an astonishment; and these nations shall serve the King of Babylon seventy years" (Jeremiah 25:11).

The nations referred to are all those who were planning (against God's message) to surrender to Nebuchadnezzar. These include Egypt, the land of Uz, all Kings of the land of the Philistines, Ashkelon, Azzah, Ekron, the remnants of Ashdod, Edom, Moab, the children of Ammon, and the Kings of Tyrus/Tyre, Zidon, and Arabia. All were asked to put their necks in Nebuchadnezzar's yoke to live:

> *And it shall come to pass, that the nation and Kingdom which will not serve the same Nebuchadnezzar the King of Babylon, and that will not put their neck under the yoke of the king of Babylon, that nation will I punish . . . with the sword, and with the famine, and with the pestilence, until I have consumed them by his hand. Therefore, hearken not to your prophets . . . for they prophesy a lie unto you . . . and that I should drive you out, and ye should perish. But the nations that bring their neck under the yoke of the King of Babylon, and serve him, those will I let remain still in their land. . .. And they shall till it and dwell therein.*
> Jeremiah 27:8-11

The yoke referred to is supposed to be a wooden one, which Jeremiah— in obedience to God's message—made and wore around his neck. However, when Hananiah made a false prophecy, saying that God had broken the yoke of the King of Babylon, and attacked Jeremiah, breaking the wooden yoke around his neck, God became angry and proclaimed Hananiah's demise (Jeremiah 28:1-4). He died within six months.

Hereafter, God also changed his mind. Instead of a wooden yoke around their neck, he would make it an iron yoke for all the nations conspiring against Nebuchadnezzar (Jeremiah 28:13-14). Had they obeyed God's words, bearing the wooden yoke and surrendering, they could have lived—and the destruction of the temple might have been avoided.

Even when the Lord commanded Judah (and the other nations

conspiring against Nebuchadnezzar) to put their neck under his yoke, he was already planning for their return after seventy-year-long captivity. God's divine love and mercy for his chosen people remained undeterred, as reflected in the following covenant:

> And it shall come to pass when the seventy years are accomplished, that I will punish the King of Babylon, and that nation, saith the Lord, for iniquity, and the hand of the Chaldeans, and will make it perpetual desolations.
> Jeremiah 25:12

The promise of the return states:

> After seventy years be accomplished at Babylon, I will visit you and perform good toward you, in causing you to return to this place. For I know the thoughts I have toward you. . .. Of peace, and not of evil, to give an unexpected end. . .. I will turn away your captivity, and I will gather you from all the Nations, and from all the places whither I have driven you . . . and I will bring you again unto the place whence I caused you to be carried away captive.
> Jeremiah 29:10-14

The Lord God made a new covenant with his chosen people:

> Behold, the days come, saith the Lord, that I will make a new covenant with the house of Israel, and with the house of Judah: Not according to the covenant that I made with your fathers...I will put my laws in their inward parts, and write it in their hearts; and will be their God, and they shall be my people.
> Jeremiah 31:31-33

This covenant seems to be the culmination of God's covenant-making with Israel: "It may be viewed as a document of God's prophetic program and of his policies of the administration."[89] The new covenant made the Sinaitic covenant obsolete, and it serves as a moral and civic guide for Israel and the pre-Christian era. The present laws will not be written on stones but, rather, in the hearts and minds of God's people. They will, in short, conform in all respects to the moral codes of Scripture. Instead of being external obedience to the law, it's now internalized. While under the Sinaitic covenant, only the Israelites were regarded as God's people. But the new covenant covers all believers as God's people, *his people.*

Even after the fall of Judah and the deportation to Babylon, God continued to send his prophetic messages to the Exiles in Babylon—though not to those who were left behind, commanded by the Lord to stay in the land or surrender to Nebuchadnezzar but not to go to Egypt. However, they disobeyed and fled to other places, including Egypt. The people who fled to Egypt never returned to the land of Judah; they all perished in Egypt because they drowned in the swamp of idolatry in that country.

But in keeping with God's redemptive administration of justice to his chosen people, after they were in captivity for seventy years, he launched his divine and sovereign power, stirring the heart of Cyrus.[90] He issued the decree that restored Judah to its promised homeland in 538 B.C. (Jeremiah 25:11-12; 2 Chronicles 36:22-23).

From this time forward, all the Jewish captives that had been scattered about in all the cities and regions of the Persian Empire gathered and prepared to return to the Promised Land on three different occasions.

The first return occurred in 537/536 B.C. It was led by Zerubbabel, grandson of Jehoiachin,[91] who was appointed a governor of Judah; Joshua, the son of Jozadak, was the high priest (Ezra 2:1-63; Haggai 1:1).

One of the reasons the Lord stirred Cyrus' spirit was to build the house of the Lord in Jerusalem. Cyrus, therefore, ordered the general public to

---

[89] Hindson, 2013, *text and annotation*, 31:31-34, page 1109; Jeremiah 31:31-34, pg. 1109

[90] Narrative citation Dr. Ayuba Mshelia (Wikipedia, 2020) (Personal communication), Cyrus became King after the defeat of the Babylonians by the Persian army on October 12, 539 BC, but he didn't enter until October 29, 539 BC.

[91] Narrative citation Dr. Ayuba Mshelia (2020) (Personal communication), According to early Jewish historians; but modern scholars seems to agree that he might have succeeded Sheshbazzar.

freely donate their silver, gold, goods, and beasts toward that goal. The total number of those who returned at this time was around 49,897, including 4,289 priests and 341 Levites.

King Cyrus gave out the articles of the house of the Lord that Nebuchadnezzar had brought to Babylon. This included 30 gold dishes, 1,000 silver dishes, 29 knives, 30 gold bowls, and 410 silver bowls; in short, Sheshbazzar returned with a total of 5,400 articles of gold and silver (Ezra 1:11). The rebuilding of the new temple was completed in 516 B.C. It was called Zerubbabel Temple and, for five hundred years, it served as the spiritual center of Israel.

King Cyrus appointed Zerubbabel governor, not King, in Judah. This meant that the human kindship of Israel and Judah ended in the sixth century BC, with the deportation of Zedekiah. It did not contradict or betray the curse on Jehoiachin. Even if he had not been restored by Nebuchadnezzar's son Evil-Merodach, King of Persia, on the twenty-seventh day of the twelfth month in the thirty-seventh year of his exile (2 King 25:27).

Evil-Merodach became King of Babylon on the 25th day of the 12th month, inheriting the throne from his father around 560 B.C. The new King made him change his prison clothes, and he allowed him to have all his meals in the King's presence all the remaining days of his life. His throne was also set above the thrones of other Kings in the empire. He was provided with all he needed, including a regular allowance "by the King, a portion for each day, all the days of his life" (2 Kings 25:27-30).

Even though Jesus' ancestry through Joseph includes Jehoiachin/Jeconiah (Matthew 1:11-16), the line of descent is recorded merely to show Jesus' right to the throne of David. This is because of Jesus' Virgin birth (Matthew 1:18; Luke 1:34-36). Thus, because Jesus was not the natural son of Joseph, "the pronouncement against Jehoiachin line is not contradicted."[92] Jesus' human descent is traced through Mary, a descendant of King David through his son Nathan. Christ "did not abrogate the prophetic curse against Jehoiachin's line, rather confirming the veracity and worthiness of the Scripture are again demonstrated."[93]

The second return occurred in 458 B.C., 79 years after the first. It

Hindson, 2013, *text and annotation*, 22:30, page 1095
[93] Hindson, 2013, pg. *Ibid*

was led by Ezra, the priest, and scribe (Ezra 7:1-10). Its purpose was the full recovery of the Temple-centered worship of covenantal faith. This was to replenish the materials needed to restore the official sacrifices in the Temple.

With this second return, Ezra brought with him lots of gifts of gold, silver, wheat, baths of wine (2,200 L), 100 baths of oil, and more from King Ahasuerus/Artaxerxes, his princes, and his counselors, which were freely given (Ezra 7:15). He also brought along utensils for the service of the house of the Lord from the royal treasury and presented them in full before God (Ezra 7:19-20). The number of males who returned with Ezra this time was around 1,775, with two priests and 38 Levites.

The third and final return occurred in 444 B.C., 14 years after the second, under the leadership of Nehemiah ("The Lord comforts"), the son of Hachaliah, King Artaxerxes' personal cupbearer (Nehemiah 1:1, 11). Nehemiah was appointed a governor of Judah, and he served as such for twelve years.

According to Nehemiah, the decree was given to him in the twentieth year of King Artaxerxes's reign, in the month of Nissan (March–April), and it lasted up to the thirty-second year of King Artaxerxes's reign (Nehemiah 2:1-10; 5:14; 13:6). The purpose of this return was to restore the city, rebuilding the walls of Jerusalem and restoring the peoples' fortunes (Nehemiah 1:5-11; 2:5-8).

The number who returned at this time was only one: Nehemiah (Nehemiah 2:1-11). The King provided Nehemiah with the building materials. The building and restoration of the walls were completed in a record time—fifty-two days—on the twenty-fifth day of the sixth month (Nehemiah 6:15). The people celebrated the Feast of Booths in the seventh month. They gathered to repent and to place seals on the document of the covenant on the twenty-fourth day of the seventh month, and they celebrated the dedication of the wall itself much later to get the city repopulated for the event (Nehemiah 8:13-18; 9:1-38; 12:27-43).

No foreigner was allowed to attend these events (Neh.13:1-3). Nehemiah was able to accomplish this because of his constant prayer to the Lord. He also initiated many social, political, and religious reforms among the people (Nehemiah 5:1-9).

After a brief visit to Persia in 433 B.C.), he returned to Jerusalem in 432

B.C.) and dealt with further matters of religious and social reforms, such as expelling Tobiah from his lucrative and corrupt position in the Temple, restoring the Levites who had forsaken their posts and left their service, mankind the people observe the Sabbath day properly, and chastising those who'd intermarried with foreign women (Nehemiah 13:4-13).

According to an interpretation of Prophet Daniel's seventy-weeks prophesy, from the date of the annunciation of the decree in 444 B.C. to the Messiah, a period of seven weeks and threescore and two weeks, or 483 years, would transpire.[94] [95]

Daniel 9:26 says that after threescore and two weeks shall the Messiah be cut off. This refers to the Crucifixion, which probably occurred in April of 32 AD. According to the interpretation presented in the KJV, this means the first seven weeks (with a week equaling seven years) had already transpired, which left us with 483 years (70 x 7 = 490 - 7 = 483). The calculation is based on Daniel's use of a prophetical year (360 days) rather than a solar year (365 days).

God stirred the heart of Cyrus, the King of Persia, showing us he had not forgotten his earlier promise to his own people. That promise said that, after seventy years of servitude to the gentile Kingdom of the Babylonians, the Lord would get his people out. He would punish them—even if it meant sending them to serve a gentile King—but his divine love and abundant mercy would still be with them . . . just as he had kept them in the wilderness for forty years before bringing them to the land he'd promised to their forefathers.

The third period of the genealogy of Christ can be divided into historical periods spanning five dominions or Empires: Persian domination after Nehemiah's reforms (432–331 B.C.), Greek/Hellenistic (331–164 B.C.), the Maccabean Revolution (167–142 B.C.), the Hasmonean Dynasty (142–63 B.C.), and the Roman Empire (63–4 B.C.; Jesus was born around 4 or 5 B.C.).[60]

During these intervening periods, there was a dark age in Israel between the completion of the Zerubbabel Temple and Nehemiah's city walls, which spanned some 400 years until the coming of Christ, when

---

[94] Hindson, 2013, *text and annotation*, 9:24-9:26, page 1248-1250
[95] Doctrinal Footnote 9:24, pg. 1249. 70 x 7= 490-7 = 483; seventy weeks each is equivalent to 7 years, less one year (one week already transpired).

prophecy seemed to cease altogether. Nothing, Park, 2014 argued, was Scripturally recorded. However, despite the gloom in prophecy, God kept going with his administration of redemptive plan for mankind until the fullness of time, when he sent his only begotten Son in the flesh as the Messiah/Mashiach through the seed of a woman (Genesis 3:15; Galatians 4:4). The genealogy of Christ is not necessarily a genealogy according to the flesh, the purpose of which is to record every generation without omission. Christs' genealogy is a covenantal genealogy that reveals God's providential administration in the history of redemption. Thus, the promise of the eternal covenant is intimately related to the covenantal genealogies that describe and preserve the pure lineage through which he would come as the Messiah to save "the Elect" and all of humanity.

It is only divinely befitting that Jesus Christ authenticates the angel through whom he has given this revelation to John, in which he states:

> *I have sent mine angel to testify unto you these things in the Churches. I am the root and offspring of David and the bright and morning star.*
> Rev. 22:16

This means Jesus is the fulfillment of the Messianic promise of Isaiah (11:1), the fulfillment of the promises to Abraham, and the fulfillment of the promises to David (Genesis 12:2-3, 2 Samuel 7:16-18; Isaiah 11:12; Luke 1:31-33). Referring to him as "the bright and morning star" implies his imminent coming in the New Age, the Messianic Millennium Kingdom (Rom. 13:11,12; 2 Pet. 1:19).[96] [97]

---

[96] Hindson, 2013, text and annotation, 22:16,17, pg. 1934
[97] ibid, Doctrinal footnotes 5:3, pg. 18

MESSIANIC GENEALOGY BIBLIOGRAPHY

"1 Chronicles 3:5" (2020) *The International Bible Society* retrieved [Online] from (https://www.biblica.com/bible/?osis=niv:1chronicles.3:5-3:5);

"1 Enoch 10:11-12" retrieved [Online] from (http://www.ccel.org/c/charles/otpseudepig/enoch/ENOCH_1.HTM#10_12).

"1 Kings 21:21-29" (2020) *The International Bible Society* retrieved [Online] from (https://www.biblica.com/bible/?osis=niv:1

"1chronicles 6:3-14" (2020) *The International Bible Society* retrieved [Online] from (https://.biblica.com/bible?osis=niv:1chronicles.6:3-6:14).

"Aaron" (2020) *Wikipedia* retrieved [Online] from https://en.wikipedia.org/wiki/Aaron

"Abijah of Judah" (2020) *Familypedia* retrieved [Online] from https://familypedia.wikia.org/wiki/Abijah_of_Judah

"Ahaz" (2020) *Wikipedia* retrieved [Online] from Ahaz-Wikipedia' *en.m.wikipedia.org*

"Ahaziah of Judah" (2020) *Wikipedia* retrieved [Online] from https://en.wikipedia.org/wiki/Ahaziah_of_Judah

"Amaziah of Judah" (2020) *Wikipedia* retrieved [Online] from https://en.wikipedia.org/wiki/Amaziah_of_Judah

"Amminadab" (2020) *Wikipedia* retrieved [Online] from https://en.wikipedia.org/wiki/Amminadab

"Amon of Judah" (2020) *Wikipedia* retrieved [Online] from https://en.wikipedia.org/wiki/Amon_of_Judah

"Arpachshad" (2020) *Wikipedia* retrieved [Online} from https://en.wikipedia.org/wiki/Arpachshad

"Asa of Judah" (2020) *Wikipedia* retrieved [Online] from https://en.wikipedia.org/wiki/Asa_of_Judah

"Biblical Theology Bulletin", 35 (2): 43-50, doi: 10.1177/01461079050350020201 (https://doi.org/10.1177%2F01461079050350020201).

"Boaz" (2020) *Wikipedia* retrieved [Online] from https://en.wikipedia.org/wiki/Boaz

"Book of Jubilees" (2020) *Wikipedia,* retrieved [Online} from https://en.wikipedia.org/wiki/Book_of_Jubilees

"Caffeine for masses" retrieved [Online] from http://caffeine4masses.blogspot.com/2013/12/

"Curse of Ham" (2020) *Wikipedia* retrieved [Online] from https://en.wikipedia.org/wiki/Curse_of_Ham

"Deuteronomy 29:20" *New International Version,* retrieved [Online] from (https://www.biblica.com/bible/?osis=niv:Deateronomy.29:20-29:20).

"Easton's Bible Dictionary" (2020) *Biblestudytools* retrieved [Online] from https://www.Biblestudytools.com/dictionaries/eastons-bible-Dictionary/

"Eber" (2020) *Wikipedia* retrieved [Online} from https://en.wikipedia.org/wiki/Eber

"Epistle to the Hebrews" (2020) retrieved [Online] from Epistle to the Hebrews - Wikipedia

"Esli ben Nagge" (2020) *Familypedia* retrieved [Online] from https://familypedia.wikia.org/wiki/Esli_ben_Nagge

"Exodus 20:5" (2020) *The International Bible Society* retrieved [Online] from (https://www.biblica.com/bible/?osis=niv:Exodus.20:5-20:5,

"Ezra's genealogy in Ezra 7:1-5" (2020) *The International Bible Society* retrieved [Online] from (https://www.biblica.com/bible?osis=niv:Ezra.7:1-7:5)

"Genealogy of Jesus" (2020) retrieved [Online} from https://en.wikipedia.org/wiki/genealogy_of_Jesus, pg. 6/21

"Genealogy of Jesus", *Wikipedia* November 28, 2020, retrieved [Online] from (https://en.wikipedia.org/wiki/genealogy_of_Jesus, page 6/21

"Genesis 11:22" (2020) *Biblestudytools,* retrieved [Online} from https://www.Biblestudytools.com/genesis/11-22.html

"Genesis 4:24" (2020) *Biblestudytools*, retrieved [Online] https://www. Biblestudytools.com/genesis/4-24.html

"Hezekiah" (2020) *Wikipedia* retrieved [Online] from https://en.wikipedia. org/wiki/Hezekiah

"Hitchcocks Bible Dictionary" (2020) *Biblestudytools* retrieved [Online] from https://www.Biblestudytools.com/dictionaries/ hitchcocks-bible-names/

"Jacob" (2020) *Wikipedia* retrieved [Online} from https://en.wikipedia. org/wiki/Jacob

"Jared (biblical figure)" *Wikipedia* (2020) retrieved [Online] from https:// en.wikipedia.org/wiki/Jared_(biblical_figure)

"Jeconiah" (2020) *Wikipedia* retrieved [Online] from https://en.wikipedia. org/wiki/Jeconiah

"Jehoahaz of Judah" (2020) *Wikipedia* retrieved [Online] from https:// en.wikipedia.org/wiki/Jehoahaz_of_Judah

"Jehoiakim" (2020) *Wikipedia* retrieved [Online] from https://en.wikipedia. org/wiki/Jehoiakim

"Jehoram of Judah" (2020) *Wikipedia* retrieved [Online] from https:// en.wikipedia.org/wiki/Jehoram_of_Judah

"Johanan" (2020) Wikipedia, retrieved [Online] from https://en.wikipedia. org/wiki/Johanan_(High_Priest)

"Josiah" (2020) *Wikipedia* retrieved [Online] from https://en.wikipedia. org/wiki/Josiah

"Jotham of Judah" (2020) *Familypedia* retrieved [Online] from https:// familypedia.wikia.org/wiki/Jotham_of_Judah/descendants

"Judah" {Son of Jacob} (2020) *Wikipedia* retrieved [Online] from https:// en.wikipedia.org/wiki/Judah_(son_of_Jacob)

"Jude, Epistle of" (2020) *Biblestudytools.com* retrieved {Online} from https:// www.Biblestudytools.com/dictionaries/smiths-bible-Dictionary/jude-epistle-of.html

"Mahalaleel" (2020) *The International Bible Society* retrieved [Online] from https://en.wikipedia.org/wiki/Mahalalel

"Manasseh of Judah" (2020) *Wikipedia* retrieved [Online] from https:// en.wikipedia.org/wiki/Manasseh_of_Judah

"Manasseh" (2020) *Encyclopedia Britannica* retrieved [Online] from *https:// www.britannica.com/biography/Manasseh-king-of-Judah*

"Mary's Genealogy & the Talmud" retrieved [Online] from (https://web.
    archive.org/web/20090323155324/http://www..frontline-apologetics.
    com/mary_genealogy_talmud.html); archived from the original
    (http://www.frontline-apologetics.com/mary_genealogy_talmud.
    html).

"Matthew 18:21-22" (2020) *Biblestudytools*, retrieved [Online] from https://
    www.Biblestudytools.com/matthew/passage/?q=matthew+18:21-22

"Methuselah" (2020) *Wikipedia*, retrieved {Online} from https://
    en.wikipedia.org/wiki/Methuselah

"Nabal" (2020) *Wikipedia* retrieved [Online] from https://en.wikipedia.
    org/wiki/Nabal

"Nahor son of Terah" (2020) *Wikipedia* retrieved {Online} from https://
    en.wikipedia.org/wiki/Nahor,_son_of_Terah

"Nahshon" (2020) *Wikipedia* retrieved [Online] from https://en.wikipedia.
    org/wiki/Nahshon

"Obed {biblical}" (2020) *Wikipedia* retrieved [Online] from https://
    en.wikipedia.org/wiki/Obed_(biblical_figure)

"Ram" (2020) *Wikipedia* retrieved [Online] from https://en.wikipedia.org/
    wiki/Ram_(biblical_figure)

"Rehoboam" (2020) *Wikipedia* retrieved [Online] from https://en.wikipedia.
    org/wiki/Rehoboam

"Romans 1:3" *Biblica* retrieved [Online] from (https://www.biblica.com/
    bible/?osis=niv:Romans

"Salmon" (2020) *Wikipedia* retrieved [Online] from https://en.wikipedia.
    org/wiki/Salmon_(biblical_figure)

"Serug" (2020) *Biblestudytools* retrieved [Online] from https://www.
    Biblestudytools.com/Dictionary/serug/

"Shuah" (2020) *Wikipedia* retrieved [Online] from https://en.wikipedia.
    org/wiki/Shuah

"Smith Bible Dictionary" (2020) *Biblestudytools* retrieved
    [Online] from https://www.Biblestudytools.com/dictionaries/
    smiths-bible-Dictionary/

"Solomon" (2020) *Wikipedia* retrieved [Online] from https://en.wikipedia.
    org/wiki/Solomon

"The Problem of the Curse on Jeconiah in Relation to the Genealogy of
    Jesus – Jews for Jesus" *Jews for Jesus*, 1 January 2005.retrieved [Online]

from (https://jewsforjesus.org/answers/the-problem-of-the-curse-on-jeconiah-in-relation-to-the-genealogy-of-jesus-issues-prpphecy/)

"Zachariah 12:12" retrieved [Online] from (https://www.biblica.com/bible/?osis=:Zachariah.12:12-12:12).

"Zedekiah" (2020) *Wikipedia* retrieved [Online] from https://en.wikipedia.org/wiki/Zedekiah

"Zerubbabel" (2020) Wikipedia, retrieved [Online] from Zerubbabel - Wikipedia

Albright, William F. & Mann, C.S (1971), Matthew: A New Translation with Introduction and Commentary. *The Anchor Bible*, 26, New York, New York: Doubleday & co, ISBN 978-0-385-08658-5.

Bauckham, Richard (1995); Tamar's Ancestry and Rehab's Marriage: Two Problems in the Matthean Genealogy, *Novum Testamentum*, 37 (4): 313-329, doi: 10.1163/1568536952663168 (https://doi.org/10.1163%2F1568536952663168).

Bauckham, Richard (2004). Jude and the relatives of Jesus in the Early Church, London, England: *T&T Clark International*, pgs. 315-373. ISBN 978-0-567-08297-8

Bengel, J. A. (1860) *Gnomon of the New Testament*, vol. 1 Philadelphia, PA: Smith, English and Co., 87.

Blair, Harold A. (1964), "Matthew 1, 16 and the Matthean Genealogy", *Studia Evangelica*, 2: 149-54.

Borg, Marcus J., and Crossan, John Dominic (2009) *The First Christmas What the Gospels Really Teach about Jesus's Birth Paperback,* San Francisco, California: HarperOne

Brown, R.E. (1977) *the Birth of the Messiah*, New York, New York: Doubleday Publishing

Crane, F, Dr. (1926) *the Lost Books of the Bible and the Forgotten Books of Eden (1926),* 16th Edition, Cleveland, Ohio: The World Publishing Company

Damascene, John (N.A.) an Exact Exposition of the Orthodox Faith. Book 1V Chapter X1V: Concerning our Lord's genealogy and concerning the Holy mother of God. retrieved [Online] from (http://www.orthodox.net/fathers/exactiv.html)

France, R.T. (1985) *the Gospel According to Matthew: An Introduction and Commentary*, Grand Rapids, Michigan: WM B. Eerdmans Publishing ISBN978-0-8028-3549-9

Green, J.B., McKnight, S. Marshall, I.H. (1992), Dictionary of Jesus and the Gospels: A Compendium of Contemporary Biblical Scholarship retrieved [Online] from (https://books.google.com/books?id=9ntwNm-toogC&pg=PA254#v=snippet&q=%22Matthew%20begins%20his%20Gospel%22&f=false). Inter Varsity Press, pgs.254-259, ISBN 0-8308-1777-8.

Gundry Robert H (1982), Matthew: A Commentary on his Literary and Theological art retrieved [Online] from (https://archive.org/details/matthewcommentar00gund_1).

Herbermann, Charles (ed.), *Catholic Encyclopedia*. New York, New York: Robert Appleton Company.

Hervey, Arthur Charles (1853), *The Genealogies of Our Lord and savior Jesus Christ*, Cambridge, MA: Macmillan and Co. retrieved [Online] from (https://books.google.com/?id=l8NhHThXtbEC).

Hervey, Lord A.C. (1853), *The Genealogies of Our Lord and Savior Jesus Christ*, Cambridge, England: Macmillan and Co.

Hindson, E. (2013) *King James Version (K.J.V.,), Study Bible*, Second Edition, Nashville, TN: Thomas Nelson Publishers

Hutchinson, John C. (2001), "Women, Gentiles, and the Messianic Mission in Matthew's Genealogy", Bibliotheca Sacra, 158; 152-164

Ignatius of Antioch, Epistle to the Ephesians, p. 18 retrieved [Online] from (http://www.ccel.org/ccel/schaff/anf01.v.ii.xviii.html).

Irenaeus, Adversus haereses ("Against Heresies"), p.3.22.3 retrieved [Online] from (http://www.ccel.org/ccel/schaff/anf01.ix.iv.xxiii.html#ix.iv.xxiii-p10)

Jacobi, Doctrina p. 1.42 (PO 40.67–68) retrieved [Online] from (http://www.patristique.org/IMG/pdf/PO_40_VIII_5.pdf)) Translated in part by Williams, A. Lukyn (1935), Adversus Judaeos: a bird's-eye view of Christian apologiae until the Renaissance (https:// books.google.com/?id=6m43AAAAIAAJ&pg=PA155), Cambridge University Press, pp. 155–156, OCLC 747771 (http s://www.worldcat.org/oclc/747771)

Johnson, M. D. (1988), *The Purpose of the Biblical genealogies (2nd ed.)*, Cambridge, England: Cambridge University Press, pg. 142, ISBN 978-0-521-35644-2.

Juel, Donald (1992), *Messianic Exegesis: Christological Interpretation of the Old Testament in Early Christianity*, Philadelphia, PA: Fortress Press, pgs. 59-88, ISBN 978-0-8006-2707-2

Lightfoot, John (1663), *Horae Hebraicae et Talmudicae*, Published 1859, pg. 55, retrieved [Online] from (http://philologos.org/_eb-jl/luke03.htm), 3

Lumpkin, Joseph B. (2011) *The Books of Enoch: A Complete Volume Containing 1 Enoch (The Ethiopic Book of Enoch), 2 Enoch (The Slavonic Secrets of Enoch), 3 Enoch (The Hebrew Book of Enoch)* 2nd Edition. Julian, PA: Fifth Estate, Incorporated;

Maas, Anthony (1913): "Genealogy of Christ" retrieved [Online] from (*https://en.wikisource.org/wiki/Catholic_Encyclopedia_{1913}/Genealogy_of_Christ*)

Maas, Anthony. (October 9, 2013) "Genealogy (in the Bible)". *The Catholic Encyclopedia,* Vol.6. New York: Robert Appleton Company, retrieved [Online] from (http://www.newadvent.org/cathen/06408a.htm).

Maloney C. M. and Robert, P. "The Genealogy of Jesus: Shadows and lights in his past", America, December 17, 2007 retrieved [Online] from (http://americamagazine.org/issue/638/faith-focus/genealogy-jesus).

Marcus J. Borg and John Dominic Crossan (2009), *the First Christmas*, New York, New York: Harper Collins

Marshall D. Johnson. (2002) *the purpose of the Biblical Genealogies with Special Reference to the setting of the Genealogies of Jesus* Eugene, Oregon: Wipf and Stock Publishing

Martyr, Justin, Dialogus cum Tryphone Judaeo (n.a) Dialogue with Trypho, pg. 100 retrieved [Online] from (http://www.ccel.org/ccel/schaff/anf01.viii.iv.c.html)

Nolland, John (1997), "Jechoniah and His Brothers" (PDF), *Bulletin for Biblical Research,* Bible studies, 7: 169-78. retrieved [Online] from (https://www.biblicalstudies.org.uk/pdf/genealogy_nolland.pdf)

Nolland, John (1997). "Jechoniah and His Brothers" retrieved [Online] from (http://www.biblicalstudies.org.uk/pdf/genealogy_nolland.pdf (PDF). Bulletin for Biblical Research, Bible studies, 7:169-178

Nolland, John (2005): The Gospel of Matthew: A commentary on the Greek text, Grand Rapids, Colorado: W.B. Eerdmans, pgs.65- 87. ISBN978-0-8028-2389-2

Oxford, C. (1995) Book of Enoch retrieved [Online] from http://www. ccel.org/c/charles/otpseudepig/enoch/ENOCH_1.HTM#10_12

Pamphilius, Eusebius (1890), Eusebius Pamphilius: Church History, Life of Constantine, V11, New York, New York: Christian Literature Publishing co. retrieved [Online] from http://www.ccel.org/ccel/ schaff/npnf201.html

Park, Abraham (2010) *The Unquenchable lamp of the Covenant, The first Fourteen Generations in the Genealogy of Jesus Christ,* Singapore: Periplus Publishing

Park, Abraham (2014) *The Promise of the Eternal Covenant: God's Profound Providence as revealed in the Genealogy of Jesus Christ (The Post-Exilic Period)* North Clarendon, Vermont: Periplus Editions publishers

Robertson, A.T., (2020) "Commentary on Luke 3:23, *Biblestudytools,* retrieved [Online] from (http://www.Biblestudytools.com/ commentaries/robertsons-word-pictures/luke/luke-3-23.html)

Schaff, Philip (1882) "Tertullian, De carne Christi (On the flesh of Jesus Christ)", pgs. 20-22, retrieved [Online] from (http://www.ccel.org/ ccel/schaff/anf03.v.vii.xx.html).

Schaff, Philip (1882). *The Gospel According to Matthew*, New York, New York: Charles Scribner's Sons, ISBN 0-8370-9740-1.

Schaff, Philip NF1-06. St. Augustine: Sermon on the Mount; Harmony of the Gospels; Homilies on the Gospels, pgs. 2.1.2-4 retrieved [Online] from (http://www.ccel.org/ccel/schaff/npnf106.vi.v.ii.html)

Schaff, Philip NF1-06. St. Augustine: Sermon on the Mount; Harmony of the Gospels; Homilies on the Gospels, pgs. 16-21, retrieved [Online] from (http://www.ccel.org/ccel/schaff/npnf106.vi.v.ii.html)

Sextus Julius Africanus (n.a.). Epistula ad Aristidem *Epistle to Aristides:* retrieved [Online] from (http://www.ccel.org/ccel/schaff/ anf06.v.iii.i.html).

Silvertsen, Barbara (2005), "New testament genealogies and the families of Mary and Joseph" retrieved [Online] from (http:// www.thefreelibrary.com/New+testament+genealogies+and +the+families+of+Mary+and+Joseph-a0133946349,

Sparks, James T. (2008) *The Chronicler's Genealogies*, Atlanta, GA: Society of Biblical Literature

Stothert, Rev. Richard (N.A.)St. Augustin: Reply to Faustum the Manichaean, [Contra Faustum Manichaeum], A.D. 400) retrieved [Online] from (http://www.ccel.org/ccel/schaff/npnf104.iv.ix.i.html)

Wierwille, Victor Paul (2006) Jesus Christ Our Promised Seed, New Knoxville, OH: American Christian Press, pgs. 113-132

APPENDIX A – TABLE 1

Patrilineage of Jesus Christ according to Matthew 1:1-16

GOD				
1. Adam	15. Heber	29. Naasson/ Nahshon	43. Ahaz	57. Eleazar
2. Seth	16. Phalec	30. Salmon and Rahab/ Rachab	44. Hezekiah	58. Matthan
3. Enos	17. Ragau	31. Boaz and Ruth	45. Manasseh	59. Jacob
4. Cainan	18. Saruch	32. Obed	46. Amon	60. Joseph
5. Maleleel	19. Nachor	33. Jesse	47. Josiah	61. Jesus
6. Jared	20. Thara/ Terah	34. David and Bathsheba	48. Jeconiah/ Jehoaichin	
7. Enoch	21. Abraham	35. Solomon	49. Shealtiel	
8. Mathusala	22. Isaac	36. Rehoboam	50. Zerubbabel	
9. Lamech	23. Jacob	37. Abijah	51. Abihud	
10. Noah	24. Judah and Tamar	38. Asa	52. Eliakim	
11. Shem	25. Phares/ Perez	39. Jehoshaphat	53. Azor	
12. Arphaxad	26. Esrom/ Hezron	40. Jehoram	54. Zadok	
13. Cainan	27. Aram/Ram	41. Uzziah/ Azariah	55. Achim	
14. Shelah	28. Amminadab	42. Jotham	56. Eliud	

APPENDIX B - TABLE 2

Patrilineage of Jesus Christ according to Luke 3:23-38

GOD				
1. Adam	17. Ragau	33. Jesse	49. Er	65. Esli
2. Seth	18. Saruch	34. David	50. Elmodam	66. Naum
3. Enos	19. Nachor	35. Nathan	51. Cosam	67. Amos
4. Cainan	20. Thara/ Terah	36. Mattatha	52. Addi	68. Mattathias
5. Maleleel	21. Abraham	37. Menan	53.Melchi	69. Josseph
6. Jared	22. Isaac	38. Melea	54. Neri	70.Jannai
7. Enoch	23. Jacob	39. Eliakim	55. Salathiel	71. Melchi
8. Mathusala	24. Judah	40. Jonam	56. Zorobabel	72. Levi
9. Lamech	25. Phares/ Perez	41. Joseph	57. Rhesa	73. Matthat
10. Noah	26. Esrom/ Hezron	42. Judah	58. Joannan	74. Heli
11. Shem	27. Aram/Ram	43. Simeon	59. Juda/Joda	75. Joseph
12. Arphaxad	28. Amminadab	44. Levi	60. Joseph	76. Jesus
13. Cainan	29. Naasson/ Nahshon	45. Matthat	61. Semei	
14. Shelah	30. Salmon	46. Jorim	62. Mattathias	
15. Heber	31. Boaz	47. Eliezer	63.Maath	
16. Phalec	32. Obed	48. Jose	64. Nagge	

APPENDIX C - TABLE 3

1 Chronicles 3:19-24: Generations of Zerubbabel's Descendants

Name	Zerubbabel	Hananiah	Shecaniah	Shemaiah	Neariah	Elioenal	Hodaviah
Estimated Period	570 B.C.	545 B.C.	520 B.C.	495 B.C.	470 B.C.	445 B.C.	420 B.C.

*Reckoned with an average of twenty-five years per generation. Courtesy of Park, Abraham (2014) *The Promise of the Eternal Covenant: God's Profound Providence as revealed in the Genealogy of Jesus Christ (The Post-Exilic Period)* North Clarendon, Vermont: Periplus Editions publishers

APPENDIX D - TABLE 4

A Lukan (3:23-38) Levirate Marriage Family Tree of
the Davidic Line through Solomon and Nathan

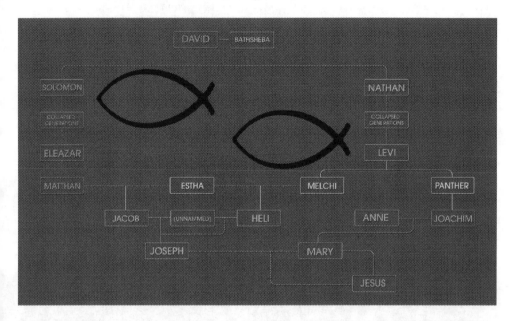

Adopted and greatly modified from "Caffeine for masses": http://
caffeine4masses.blogspot.com/2013/12/

APPENDIX E – TABLE 5

Kings Omitted in the Second Period in Matthew 1:1-16

OLD TESTAMENT 1 Chronicles 3; Appro. Reign Period*		MATTHEW 1:1-17	Luke 3:23-38
David	1010–970 BC	David	David
Solomon /Jedidiah	970–930BC	Solomon	Nathan
Rehoboam*	CR 931–914 BC	Rehoboam	Mattatha
Abijah/Abijam/Abia*	913–911	Abia	Menna
Asa	910–869 BC	Asaph	Melea
Jehoshaphat*	872–847 BC	Josaphat	Eliakim
Joram/Jehoram *	852–841 BC	Joram	Jonam
Ahaziah/Jehoahaz	841 BC	Omitted	Joseph
Athaliah (Jehoram's wife)	841–835 BC	Omitted	Omitted
Joash	835–796BC	Omitted	Judah
Amaziah*	796–767 BC	Omitted	Simeon
Azariah/Uzziah*	791–739 BC	Ozias	Levi
Jotham*	752–736	Jotham	Matthat
Ahaz*	743 BC; 736–720 BC	Achaz	Jorim
Hezekiah*	729/8–699/8 BC	Ezekias	Eliezer
Manasseh	698–643 BC	Manasses	Joshua
Amon	642–640 BC	Amos	Er
Josiah	640–609 BC	Josiah	Elmadam
Jehoahaz/Shallum	609 BC	Omitted	Cosam
Jehoiakim/Eliakim	609–598 BC	Third period	Addi
Jeconiah/Jehoiachin	598 BC	Omission	Melchi
Jechonias/Jehoiachin/Coniah		---------------	Neri
Zedekiah (last Kings of Judah)	597–586 BC	Jechonias	Shealtiel
Deported to Babylon by Nebuchadnezzar		---------------	Zerubbabel
---------- ----------- ------------------------			
- ---------- --------------------------		Salathiel	Rhesa

-------- ---------------------- ---------------	Zerubbabel	Joanan
----------- -------- -----------------------	---------------	Joda
---------- ------- ------------------------	---------------	Josech
----------------- ---------- ---------------------------	---------------	Semein
-------- ------------------------- ---------------	---------------	Mattathias
----------- -------- -----------------------	---------------	Maath
------------------------ ---------------	---------------	Naggai
------------------------ ---------------	---------------	Esli
----------------------- ---------------	---------------	Nahum
------------------------ ---------------	---------------	
-------- ----------- -----------------------	---------------	Amos
-------- ------------------------- ---------------	Abiud	Mattathias
----------- -------- -----------------------	Eliakim	Joseph
--	Azor	Jannai
--	Zadok	Melchi
--	Achim	Levi
------------------------- ---------------	Eliud	Matthat
----------- ------- -------------------------	Eleazar	Heli
--	Mathan	Joseph
--	Jacob	Jesus
--	Joseph	
--	Jesus	

*CR: Co-regency rule

APPENDIX F – TABLE 6

The Kings Omitted from the Genealogy of Jesus
Christ in the Third Period in Matthew 1:1-16

----------------- ----------------- -----------------	------------ ------------ ------------	1	2	3	4
Chronicler's Genealogy (1 Chronicles 3:15)	Josiah	Johanan	Jehoiakim (Eliakim)	Zedekiah (Mattaniah)	Jehoahaz (Shallum)
Order of Birth	Josiah	Johanan	Jehoiakim	Jehoahaz (Shallum)	Zedekiah
Order of accession)	Josiah	Jehoahaz (Shallum)	Jehoiakim (Eliakim)	Jehoiachin (Jeconiah)	Zedekiah (Mattaniah)
Matthean Genealogy (Matthew 1:10-11)	Josiah	Jehoahaz Omitted	Jehoiakim Omitted	Jeconiah Jehoiachin	Zedekiah Omitted

Adopted from Park (2014) with Modifications

Printed in the United States
By Bookmasters